Und
Human–Computer Interaction

DATE DUE FOR RETURN

ELSEVIER BUTTERWORTH-HEINEMANN INFORMATION SYSTEMS SERIES

Series Editors

Professor David Avison, BA, MSc, Phd, FBCS
Department SID
ESSEC Business School
Avenue Bernard Hirsch
BP 105
95021 Cergy-Pontoise
FRANCE

E-mail: avison@essec.fr

Professor Guy Fitzgerald, BA, MSc, MBCS
Department of Information Systems and Computing
Brunel University
Uxbridge Middlesex UB8 3PH
UK

E-mail: Guy.Fitzgerald@brunel.ac.uk

This is a new series under the Elsevier Butterworth-Heinemann imprint which will
provide medium for quality publications in the information systems field. It will also
provide continuity with the McGraw-Hill information systems series, which has been
discontinued. The new series of texts is aimed at first degree and postgraduate students,
and the global research community in information systems, computer science and
business management. Information systems is multi-disciplinary. Where formerly
emphasis was placed on the technological aspects which remain significant, it now
stresses the importance of, and the links to, the business environment particularly, in
regard to the social and organisational aspects.

If you have a book proposal for this series, please contact either of the
Series Editors.

Understanding Mobile
Human–Computer Interaction

Steve Love

ELSEVIER

BUTTERWORTH
HEINEMANN

AMSTERDAM • BOSTON • HEIDELBERG • LONDON • OXFORD • NEW YORK
PARIS • SAN DIEGO • SAN FRANCISCO • SINGAPORE • SYDNEY • TOKYO

Architectural Press
An imprint of Elsevier
Linacre House, Jordan Hill, Oxford OX2 8DP
30 Corporate Drive, Burlington, MA 01803

British Library Cataloguing in Publication Data
A catalogue record for this book is available from the British Library

ISBN 0 7506 6352 9

For information on all Elsevier Butterworth-Heinemann publications
visit our website at: http://books.elsevier.com

Typeset by Charon Tec Pvt. Ltd, Chennai, India
www.charontec.com
Printed and bound in Great Britain

Contents

To Cathy, with love

Acknowledgements

I would like to thank the following academics who have helped in the development of this book, especially Mark Turner for all his patience, guidance and suggestions for various drafts of this book. I am also grateful to Wilem-Paul Brinkman, George Ghinea, Rich Ling, Mark Lycett, Rob Macredie, Mark Perry and Rosa Scoble for the feedback and suggestions they gave me on specific chapters. Finally, I would like to thank Alfred Waller who has supported and guided me in the process of writing this book. Thanks also to the team at Elsevier Butterworth-Heinemann.

Glossary

Computer–Human Interaction	CHI
Computer Supported Collaborative Learning	CSCL
Computer Supported Collaborative Work	CSCW
Community of Practice	CoP
General Package Service	GPS
General Package Radio Service	GPRS
Global Positioning Service	GPS
Graphical User Interface	GUI
Human Centred Design	HCD
Human–Computer Interaction	HCI
Hyper Text Transfer Protocol	HTTP
Information and Communication Technology	ICT
Mobile Information Device Profile	MIDP
Pay No Attention to the Man BehInd the Curtain	PNAMBIC
Personal Digital Assistants	PDA
Short Message Service	SMS
Statistical Package for the Social Sciences	SPSS
Visual Display Terminals	VDUs
Wireless Fidelity	WiFi
Wireless Application Protocol	WAP
Wireless Local Area Network	WLAN
Wizard of Oz	WoZ
World Wide Web	WWW

1

Introduction to mobile human–computer interaction

BACKGROUND

A few years ago I was on a train travelling back to Glasgow from Edinburgh. Not long after we started the journey, the girl I was standing next to began to talk to me. I was a bit surprised as I didn't know the girl and instead of asking me something like 'how long does this train take to get to Glasgow?' she asked me how I was and what my day had been like. Although surprised, I told her I was ok; had a good day at work and that I was looking forward to watching the Scotland soccer match on TV later that evening.

As I spoke, I saw the girl starting to glare at me and as she turned away from me I heard her say 'ok, I'll call you later'. It was at this point that I realised that the girl had been talking into her hands-free mobile phone microphone and not to me. The rest of the journey continued in silence.

This example, in its own way, highlights what this book is about. Mobile communications such as mobile phones and Personal Digital Assistants

(PDAs) are influencing how we go about our daily lives from both a social and economic perspective. This book is about mobile devices and the factors you should be aware of, if you are interested in carrying out research in the area known as mobile human–computer interaction.

INTRODUCTION

This chapter aims to introduce you to the discipline of human–computer interaction (HCI). It will talk about the component disciplines of HCI and how it is an interdisciplinary subject, bringing together knowledge from different disciplines such as Psychology, Computer Science and Sociology. The chapter will also describe the various types of mobile devices that we have available to us today as well as the types of connectivity we use to get the most from these devices and mobile applications and services. The chapter finishes off with an overview of the topics that will be covered in the remaining chapters of the book.

WHAT IS HUMAN–COMPUTER INTERACTION?

The first thing we have to do is to define what is meant by the term *human–computer interaction.* For the purposes of this book HCI will be defined as the study of the relationship (*interaction*) between people and mobile computer systems and applications that they use on a daily basis. This can range from using a PDA to upload information about the HCI module you may be studying as part of your university course, to updating the credit balance on your mobile phone. Alas, right away we have to add a caveat to our definition. In the United States and countries such as Australia, New Zealand and South Africa, the term computer-human interaction (CHI) is used instead of HCI. So, if you are looking up references for a term paper or carrying out revision for your exam, this is something you should bear in mind!

So what does this term HCI actually mean, now that we have a definition before us? HCI is concerned with investigating the relationship between people and computer systems and applications. For the purposes of this book, we are concerned with understanding the users, their various capabilities and expectations and how these can be taken into consideration in the mobile system or application design. In terms of mobile systems design (or any type of design for that matter), the emphasis should always be on the users. Firstly, the system designer should set out to understand, from the outset, what the users want to use the mobile device for – what tasks they want to perform when using the system. Secondly, what characteristics of the user could have a significant effect on their performance with the system; for example, age or a physical disability such as blindness. Thirdly, once the designer has taken into consideration the needs of the users, the next stage should be to set out to develop a system that is designed to meet the needs that have been identified at the start of the process. Then the designer has to test the system in order to evaluate it to see if it meets users' needs and if they find it satisfying to use. On the basis of the feedback the designer receives at the evaluation stage, there will probably have to be an updated version of the service or application produced.

Another key aspect to this is an understanding of the environment in which the users are employing the technology (also known as *context of use*) as this can have a major impact on their ability to interact with the mobile device or application in an effective, efficient and satisfying way. For example, using your mobile phone in a dynamic environment such as the train or even walking down the street, will result in you having different requirements and expectations from your service or application. One thing you definitely want is to make sure that if you are on the train, you don't lose your wireless connection and thus not be able to update the latest sales figure on to your main database back at the office.

As can be determined from above, understanding the relationship between humans and mobile devices and applications is not necessarily an easy process. However, the aim of this book is to provide you with an insight into this process and hopefully in doing so, it will provide you with an understanding of the major factors to be considered when you are conducting your own mobile HCI research project.

DISCIPLINES INVOLVED IN MOBILE HUMAN–COMPUTER INTERACTION

Human–computer interaction is a multidisciplinary area with various academic subjects making contributions. This is a reflection of the complicated nature of an individual's interaction with a computer system. This includes factors such as an understanding of the user and the task the user wants to perform with the system, understanding of the design

tools, software packages that are needed to achieve this and an understanding of software engineering tools.

What follows is a list of some of the main disciplines involved in the
study of mobile human–computer interaction along with a brief description of the contribution each one makes to this field of study.

Psychology

Psychology has made (and continues to make) a major contribution to
the HCI discipline. Many of the research methods and system evaluation
techniques currently used in mobile HCI research are borrowed from
Psychology. For example, if you are interested in finding out people's
attitude towards using a new mobile phone-based tourist information
guide you will probably develop a questionnaire using questionnaire
design techniques that can be explained in many introductory textbooks on Psychological research methods (e.g. Coolican, 2000). As well
as attitude measures, performance measures that are used in mobile
HCI research studies (and HCI studies in general) come from the area
of experimental psychology; for example, timing how long it takes
people to complete a specific task using a mobile phone-based tourist
information guide. Information on research methods are discussed in
more detail in Chapters 4 and 5.

Understanding users and their needs is a key aspect in the design of
mobile systems, devices and applications so that they will be easy and
enjoyable to use. Individual user characteristics such as age, or personality physical disabilities such as blindness, all have an affect on users'
performance when they are using mobile applications and systems, and
these individual differences can also affect people's attitude towards the
mobile service or device that they interact with. Individual differences
and their impact on mobile HCI research and design is a topic that I will
discuss in greater detail in Chapter 3.

Computer Science

Computer Science (along with Engineering) is responsible for providing
software tools to develop the interfaces that users need to interact with
system. These include software development tools such as visual basic
and Java™ 2 Platform, Micro Edition (J2ME™).

What do these tools allow you to do? The Java™ 2 Platform, Micro Edition (J2ME™) is a software development tool that is used for the development of devices such as mobile phones and PDAs (personal digital assistants). The platform has a mobile information device profile (MIDP) whose features include what is known as end-to-end security by protecting the device against any unauthorised attempt by an outside party to access data held on your device. This is very important as you move about in a dynamic mobile environment. In addition, this platform allows you to connect and browse the internet using connection standards such as hyper text transfer protocol (http).

As well as this, MIDP has features that allow the development of user interfaces that take into consideration the limited screen space available on mobile devices and the navigational requirements necessary for usable mobile applications.

Sociology

Sociologists working in this area are responsible for looking at socio-technical aspects of HCI. For example, there is a growing body of research that has been carried out by sociologists that investigates the impact of mobile technology in social situations. For example, Ling (2002) carried out a study investigating the social impact of mobile phone use in public places. In this study he found that people perceived mobile phone use in places such as restaurants as unacceptable, partly because individuals located near mobile phone users felt coerced into eavesdropping into their conversation.

Sociologists bring methods and techniques from the social sciences (e.g. observational studies, ethnography) that can be used in the design and evaluation of mobile devices and applications. A clear example of the Sociological contribution to mobile HCI research which focuses on social usability is described in Chapter 6.

Design

People working in this area are concerned with looking at the design layout of the interface (e.g. colours, positioning of text or graphics on a screen of a PDA). This is a crucial area of mobile HCI research due to the limited screen space available for most mobile devices. Therefore, it is crucial that services and applications reflect this limitation by reducing information complexity to fit the parameters of the mobile device, without losing any substantial content.

Information systems

People who work in this area are interested in investigating how people interact with information and technologies in an organisational, managerial and business context. In an organisational context, information system professionals and researchers are interested in looking at ways in which mobile technologies and mobile applications can be used to make an organisation more effective in conducting its business on a day-to-day business. For example, if you have a team of distributed workers (e.g. photocopy machine service engineers) carrying out their daily tasks in various geographical locations, it is important that the company can harness mobile technology to co-ordinate the work activities of the team members in order to provide support in terms of scheduling appointments and providing back-up should a problem arise when the engineer is on location at a job (e.g. finding out how long it will take to order a specific part needed to fix the photocopier). This issue of the mobile worker is a topic that will be covered in more detail in Chapter 6.

As well as the mobile worker, there is the globalisation aspect to consider. For example, people across the world can have access to the internet via a mobile phone and a PDA. As a result of this, service providers need to take into consideration the cross-cultural differences in terms of beliefs and values, and the degree of technical sophistication, as these can all have an impact on the uptake and use of services.

Know Thy User

One key aspect to emerge from looking at the different disciplines involved in mobile HCI research and design is that each perspective aims to keep the user and their needs and requirements central to the work they are undertaking. Although sometimes, when you use a particular mobile application, this may not seem immediately obvious to you.

MOBILE DEVICES

Having considered some of the major disciplines which make a contribution to mobile HCI research and design, it is now worth reviewing mobile devices themselves.

Mobile phones

The growth of mobile phone usage and the development in mobile phone technology has probably had the most significant impact on the way we communicate with each other (with the exception of the internet) over the past 10 years or so. In 2003, figures released by the International Telecommunications Union (ITU), stated that there were about 1,162 million mobile telephone subscriptions worldwide. If that doesn't make an impression think about it in this way: there are probably now more people in the world who have a mobile phone subscription than those who have a landline subscription.

One factor that helped the proliferation of mobile phone use in developed societies in the late 1990s was the decreasing cost of using mobile technology (Vaananen-Vainio-Mattila and Ruska, 2000). In addition, the development of mobile telecommunications technologies such as Wireless Application Protocol (WAP) and iMode, allowed people to use their mobile phones not only to make phone calls but also to use services such as short message service (SMS), access information services from the web (e.g. news headlines) and send and receive e-mails.

Unfortunately for the mobile phone service providers, the launch of WAP-enabled mobile phones did not lead to a rush of people queuing up to buy them. There were several reasons for this. One factor which certainly impacted on the uptake by users was that WAP technology required users to dial-up to get an internet connection. This was often a slow and laborious process (not to mention the cost factor). On the other hand, iMode fared better in Japan (where the technology was originally developed) due to its ability to provide a constant internet connection for its users. Once people did get their WAP access to the internet, they found that they could only get a stripped-down version of the net, with most of the information coming in text format and a limited range of services to choose from (e.g. sports headlines, news and weather). In addition, it appeared that the service providers had not really taken into consideration the limited size of a mobile phone screen and the impact this would have on the presentation of information as well as the limited memory capacity of these phones.

However, one major social phenomenon emerged at this time – the uptake of the SMS. The popularity of 'text messaging', as it became known here in the United Kingdom, took the mobile phone service providers by surprise. It was seized upon initially by teenagers and became a fundamental way for them to maintain social relationships with their friends (Ito, 2001, Taylor and Harper, 2002). Now older sections of the population regularly use SMS texting as well. There has even been an SMS language developed to help people get round the tedium of typing with a 10-key keypad.

Despite this success, mobile phones still have challenges to overcome. These include the short battery life of the devices themselves, problems with a lack of network coverage, how to provide information to users on to a small screen without losing content, and trying to put alphabetical data into a device geared up for numerical entry.

There does, however, appear to be help at hand in the shape of 3G technology and the improved access to the internet and multi-media services it promises to offer. Discussion on the implications of 3G technology for mobile device and application development is dealt with in Chapter 8.

Personal digital assistants

Personal Digital Assistants, also known by some people as handheld PCs, were first developed with the aim of being personal electronic organisers. These devices typically contain information such as diary planners (very important for putting down information such as lecture times and appointments with supervisors), an address book and a 'to do' list. More recently, they have evolved to include some of the functionality offered by the traditional desk top PC such as word processing and they can also now provide you with access to the internet to allow you to browse the web and read your e-mail. This used to be dependent on you having cables that allowed you to connect up to the network wherever you were situated. However, PDAs now have wireless communication capabilities to allow you to transfer data (over short distances) between devices.

In terms of operating systems, there are a number available, such as Palm OS, Microsoft Windows Mobile and Symbian. However, there are some differences between these operating systems. For example, the Palm OS has been designed for PDAs which use stylus device input rather than keypad input. It is also possible to include a detachable keyboard for some of those PDAs that do not supply them. Does this seem counter-intuitive given the dynamic mobile environment in which you may be using your PDA?

Personal Digital Assistants, like mobile phones, also have their drawbacks. Battery life can be a problem as can memory capacity. For some people, relying on the handwriting capability of their PDA can be time consuming (not to mention frustrating) as they have to learn the art of using the stylus in a way that allows the system to recognise accurately what they have written.

Laptops

Laptops basically have the same functionality as desktop PCs and today they are a common feature of many people's lives. For example, when making journeys by train, it is not unusual to see people tapping away on their laptops. It is also not unusual for students to use laptops whilst they are on campus at university. However, laptops are cumbersome to use in some mobile environments. They can be bulky and have to be carried around in a case. In addition, they also have short battery lives. Unlike a mobile phone or even a PDA device, if you suddenly get the urge to use your laptop, it is not simply a case of reaching into your pocket, pulling out your laptop, and switching it on. You may have to wait while the system or the application you want to use boots up. In addition, you may have to ask the people sitting at the table next you to make space to allow you to place your laptop on the table and begin working.

Recently, there have been developments in the laptop market to try and overcome some of these technological and physical limitations. These developments have seen the launch of tablet PCs on to the market. There are two types of tablet PCs currently available. The first is known as the 'convertible tablet', which has a detachable keyboard (or in some cases a keyboard that can be folded away when not in use). The second type is known as a 'slate' tablet which does not have a keyboard and is a bit slimmer and lighter than its convertible counterpart. The slate tablet requires the user to use stylus input via a touch-sensitive screen. The convertible (as the name suggests) can also use stylus input. Both types of tablet are the same size and, like some PDAs, use wireless technology to allow the user to get access to the internet or other networks in the area they are currently located. How successful have tablets PCs been to date? That's a hard question to answer as the uptake of this technology currently appears to be quite slow. This may be due to the price (they can be more expensive than the traditional laptop) or because people are saving themselves for the development and widespread introduction of the hybrid device.

Hybrid devices

A hybrid mobile device is essentially a combination of a PDA and a mobile phone, its aim being to create a more effective mobile communication and

information device. These tend to fall into two categories. In the first category you have what is known as the 'smart phone'. A good example of
this type of device can be seen in Nokia's Communicator 9500. This device
offers users wireless connectivity, the ability to download e-mail and a
qwerty keyboard. This device is known, apparently, within the industry as
'the brick'. However, the fact that it has wireless connectivity is seen as a
big bonus for people who want to e-mail or surf the net whilst they are on
the go (all they need is a wireless network to connect to).

The second type of hybrid device is actually more similar to PDAs. A
good example of this type of device is the 'BlackBerry'. This device is
dedicated to email and is very popular with businessmen who want to
access their email whilst they are away from the office. It has a qwerty
keyboard that is relatively easy to use. This is not the most aesthetically
pleasing device to look at, but it does allow users to get access to their
e-mails. Another example of this type of device can be seen in the 'Palm
Treo 600'. This runs on the Palm operating system and offers the user all
the functionality of the PDA and has a mobile phone too. Unlike the
Blackberry, the Treo has a touch-screen and digital camera. However, the
qwerty keyboard that the Treo has is a bit smaller and more compact than
the Blackberry.

Network accessibility

There have been a number of technological developments (such as
general package services (GPS) and general package radio services
(GPRS)) that have allowed the use of mobile devices in dynamic environments (e.g. in public places such as trains or in a café). In addition,
Wireless local area networks (WLAN) have allowed laptop and PDA
users to move about a building and still maintain a network connection.
Most laptops are now equipped with WLAN cards, commonly known
as WiFi (wireless fidelity), that allow users to connect their wireless
enabled device to the internet once the user is within the range of a
transmitter. These 'hotspots', as they are known, are sometimes marked
by symbols on a wall in a street to alert other users of the opportunity
for WiFi connection. Another new form of technology which you may
have heard of, perhaps in relation to the hybrid devices mentioned
above, is 'Bluetooth' – another wireless technology that allows users who
are in close proximity to each other to exchange information between
their respective devices. Bluetooth is essentially a microchip that is fitted
into a device and it provides a short-range radio link between similarly

enabled devices. This technology is very popular for supporting voice-based applications, and it also has low power consumption (always an important factor to consider for mobile users). The next stage in technological advances that will supposedly help mobile users is 3G (discussed in Chapter 8).

STRUCTURE OF THIS BOOK

Having given you a brief introduction to the academic area of mobile HCI and discussed the various types of mobile devices and technologies that are currently available, I think it's a good time to tell you what the rest of the book is about.

In Chapter 2, I talk about individual differences. It focuses on user characteristics such as personality, cognitive skills (such as memory, spatial ability and verbal ability), age, experience of mobile technology and shows how these can affect people's attitude towards a mobile application or device. In addition, individual characteristics such as age can also have an effect on how effectively or efficiently an individual can use a mobile application.

In Chapter 3, I introduce some of the generic research methods that can be used when carrying out a mobile HCI research project. This ranges from controlled experiments in a laboratory setting to discreetly observing people's reaction to mobile phone use in public places such as cafes and restaurants. In Chapter 5, I discuss specific HCI research techniques such as a cognitive walkthrough and heuristic analysis. In both Chapters 4 and 5, I also provide technical tips, which will provide you with a step-by-step guide on how to use the methods and techniques I am discussing in each chapter.

In Chapter 5, the focus is on design issues for mobile applications and devices. The chapter starts off by discussing the importance of having a human-centred design approach to mobile product development and the stages involved in this approach. Moving on from this, I introduce some of the principles of design that you should be aware of when it comes to developing mobile applications. As well as this, there is information on several requirement gathering techniques that can be used as part of a human-centred design (HCD) approach to mobile application development. The chapter concludes by describing the main mobile prototyping techniques such as the Wizard of Oz techniques, paper and pencil testing and using mobile emulators.

In Chapter 6, I discuss the social usability aspect of mobile device use in public places. There can be no doubt that (if you remember my story at the beginning of the book) mobile devices, and in particular mobile phones, are having a significant impact on our behaviour and attitude towards the use of this type of technology in public places. I describe some of the fascinating research that is emerging from this area and offer some explanations of why we react in the way we do to mobile phone use in public places.

Chapter 7 provides you with set of guidelines to follow when you are undertaking a mobile HCI research project. This includes a discussion of ethics, a topic that is often ignored in the area of HCI, but is particularly important in the area of the mobile HCI, especially in relation to field work. This chapter also provides tips on how to conduct internet searches to find research that will help you with your project and how to present your research results in an informative way. In addition, the guidelines include tips on referencing and general presentation style.

Chapter 8 introduces the topic of data analysis. After all, it is important to analyse and interpret your research data once you have collected it. This chapter will provide examples of how to conduct data analysis based on data collection methods discussed in Chapter 3. I have adopted a step-by-step guide to using these techniques and hopefully you will be able to follow these and understand the importance of choosing the correct statistical methods for analysing your data. This is very important because if you use the wrong statistical method to assess your data, you will end up drawing the wrong conclusions about what you have found in your study.

The last chapter of the book, Chapter 9, looks at what will be the future areas of development for mobile devices and applications. Here the focus will be on the potential benefits offered by 3G technology such as the types of entertainment services that we will be able to access via of mobile device (e.g. real-time coverage of soccer matches) and how we may be able to personalise our devices even more than we can at present (e.g. an older user being able to use speech as an input method as opposed to keypad entry, which may be more cumbersome due to the small size of the buttons on the keypad). In addition, the chapter discusses the developments of location-based services where the user is able to access information which is relevant for their current context of use (e.g. tourist information guide). The chapter also discusses the need for mobile HCI researchers to move away from their current reliance on research methods that are more appropriate for lab-based research, to fully understand the context of use issues that effect people's ability to use their mobile device or application in an efficient, effective and satisfying way.

Finally, each chapter ends with a summary and provides a reference list for any research quoted within the chapter. In addition, you will be directed towards further reading, where appropriate, in order to help you gain a fuller understanding of some of the issues I have covered. There is also self test list included to prompt you to think about the main themes discussed in the chapter you have just finished reading. I have also included exercises for you to try. These are designed to help you understand (hopefully) the issues I have discussed in each chapter. You never know, they may also help you formulate your ideas for your own mobile HCI research project.

REFERENCES

Coolican, H. (2000) *Research Methods and Statistics in Psychology.* Hodder and Stoughton

Ito, M. (2001) Mobile phones, Japanese youth, and the re-placement of social contact. In *Proceedings of Annual Meeting for the Society for the Social Studies of Science*, Cambridge, MA

ITU (2003) Mobile cellular, subscribers per 100 people. http://www.itu.int/ITUD/ ict/statistics Accessed 11.01.05

Ling, R. (2002) 'The social juxtaposition of mobile telephone conversations and public spaces'. In *The Social Consequences of Mobile Telephones*, Kim, S.D. (Ed.), Chunchon, Korea

Taylor, A. and Harper, R. (2002) Age old practices in the 'new world': a study of gift-giving between teenage mobile phone users. In *Proceedings of CHI 2002*, pp. 135–446. NY: ACM Press

Vaananen-Vainio-Mattila, K. and Ruska, S. (2000) Designing mobile phones and communicators for consumers' needs at Nokia. In *Information Appliances and Beyond, Interaction Design for Consumer Products*, Eric Bergman (Ed.), San Francisco, USA: Mogan Kaufmann

SUGGESTED FURTHER READING

Preece, J., Rogers, Y., Benyon, D., Holland, S. and Carey, T. (1994) *Human– Computer Interaction*. Addison-Wesley, Chapter 2, pp. 29–52

2

User characteristics

INTRODUCTION

The aim of this chapter is to have a look at some of our individual characteristics that could have an impact on how we use, and our attitude towards, mobile applications, devices and services. This is an important area to consider because many designers of mobile information and communication technology (ICT) devices (and non-mobile ICTs for that matter) appear to have a generic user group in mind when they develop a product (Chen *et al.*, 2000). It's like a 'one size fits all' approach. Hopefully, this chapter will make you aware of the fact that there are differences between the different groups of people who use mobile device; and by being aware of their needs, designers could develop products and services that are accessible and usable to a wide range of people. The following sections provide a description of these individual characteristics and explanation of how they could have a significant effect on the user's use and perception of mobile phone devices and applications.

SPATIAL ABILITY

Spatial ability refers to the extent to which individuals can deal with spatial relations and the visualisation of spatial tasks. Real world tasks, such as learning to move through the physical environment we are in without bumping into objects (or other people), working out the trajectory of an approaching object (in order to dodge out of its way, perhaps), as well as more intellectual tasks such as designing a bridge over a river, all appear to require some degree of spatial skill. It is widely accepted that spatial ability is made up of a number of sub-factors (Carroll, 1993) and Lohman's (1989) three factor model of spatial ability is perhaps the most widely accepted. According to Lohman, spatial ability is made up of these three sub-factors:

Spatial relations: the ability to solve mental rotation problems quickly. You can see examples of these in some puzzle books. For example, you may be given a shape and asked to choose from a list of possibilities which one represents the original shape after it has been rotated by 180 degrees.

Spatial orientations: this refers to the ability of the individual to orient themselves in space relative to other people (i.e. not bumping into them). In terms of mobile HCI, we can all think of examples of people talking on their mobile phone whilst walking down the street and other people having to get out of their way. They often do not appear to be aware of the other people around them.

Visualisation: this refers to the ability to visualise the task one is currently undertaking. For example, this could be the ability to visualise the menu hierarchy that you have to navigate in order to find the information you are looking for when you use your mobile phone to find out what is showing at the local cinema.

How do you measure spatial ability? You can measure spatial ability by getting participants to complete a *psychometric test*, such as the *AH4 Group Test of General Intelligence*, Part 2 (Heim, 1970). This section of the AH4 is made up of 65 questions which are presented to the participant in a multiple choice format. Participants are given ten minutes to complete as many questions as they can and the questions are arranged in an ascending order of difficulty. The score a person obtains on this test is recognised as a measure of their spatial ability.

This ability to recognise and handle the spatial relations of objects has been significantly cited as a good predictor of performance by a number of researchers in the area of HCI (Egan 1988; Egan and Gomez, 1985). Vicente and Williges (1988) examined user performance when accessing files from within a hierarchical file structure, and found that high spatial ability users completed tasks more quickly than low spatial ability users. Vicente *et al.* (1987) conducted a study in which participants had to locate target texts from files within a hierarchical file structure. They measured a range of user characteristics and found that spatial ability emerged as the strongest predictor of time taken to locate correct texts in a retrieval system. Their results also suggested that low spatial ability users were more likely to become lost within the file system than users classed as having high spatial ability. In another study, Stanney and Salvendy (1995) found that users with low spatial ability found it difficult to construct a visual mental model of the system they were interacting with, thus leading to poor task performance.

What are the implications here for mobile applications and service design? Mobile devices have small screens and this has an impact on the amount of information that can be presented to the user at any one time. How do you go about designing a tourist information guide (with information about local cinemas, restaurants, museums, and the like) that people can access via their mobile phone or PDA, and allows them to find the information they are looking for, without making it a long process of accessing various levels until they eventually find the information they are looking for. Applying some of the research findings in relation to spatial ability and non-mobile devices, it is not hard to imagine that people with low spatial ability may find it difficult to visualise the system they are currently accessing, especially if they have to go down four or five levels, and therefore may find themselves getting confused about how to navigate back to another section of the tourist information guide. In addition, you have to remember that as people will be using these devices and applications in dynamic social environments, they will have other factors that could distract them whilst they are trying to find information. These could include things like traffic noise, people walking past (or even bumping into them) as they stand in the street, etc. Another factor to consider is the wireless connection the individual is using. If the mobile wireless connection is poor, they may find themselves standing for a long time before they can eventually find out where the restaurant they want to go for dinner is located.

PERSONALITY

The next individual difference that we will look at is personality, which is regarded by many psychologists to be our most stable individual characteristic. How would you define personality? We talk about people's personalities all the time whether it's our friends (she's a really good laugh), celebrities (they are really arrogant) or politicians (he looks really shifty). Atkinson *et al.* (1983) provide a good working definition of personality as follows: 'personality describes the characteristic patterns of behaviour and modes of thinking that determine an individual's adjustment to the environment'.

The idea that people can be classified into distinct types goes back to Hippocrates (c. 400 BC) who argued that individuals could be regarded as falling into one of four categories: choleric (irritable), melancholic (depressed), sanguine (optimistic) and phlegmatic (calm). More recently than Hoppocrates, Carl Gustav Jung (1971) who was Freud's erstwhile colleague, argued that people fall into two major categories. One group he labelled as *introverts*, who he regarded as being shy, preferring to be alone, indulging in solitary activities rather than seeking social interaction. The other group he labelled as *extroverts*, and they are seen as actively seeking the company of others and enjoying participating in group activities.

In these typologies the groups are regarded as being distinct and non-overlapping. An alternative approach to the study of personality assumes that individuals differ on a range of continuous dimensions or 'traits' where the differences between individuals are regarded as quantitative rather than categorical and quantitative. On the whole, the type approach has generally given way in personality psychology to the trait approach, as the assumption that people fall into discontinuous categories has come to seem untenable to most observers (Carver and Scheier, 1992). Relatively recently, however, a general consensus has emerged amongst trait psychologists that the basic structure of personality may only consist of five factors. Goldberg (1981) labelled these as the 'Big Five'. These are, according to McCrae and Costa (1987): extroversion, agreeableness, conscientiousness, neuroticism and openness to experience. As with spatial ability, psychologists have developed standard personality tests such as the NEO Five Factor Inventory, to measure our personality traits. In this measure, participants are asked to complete a self-report questionnaire to indicate the extent to which they agree or disagree with a number (90 in total) of statements. The statements are randomised but there are 18 statements for each of the five personality traits. Once participants complete the questionnaire their scores for each of the traits are added up to produce a score on each trait dimension.

Now that we've had an introduction to personality and how it can be measured, we must turn our attention to looking at the possible affect that personality has on people when they are interacting with ICTs.

Morgan and Macleod (1990) investigated the role of personality in a study comparing user preferences for both direct manipulation and command line interfaces. They assigned their participants to either a command line interface group or a graphical user interface group and gave them a number of tasks to complete. They measured participants' personalities using a standard personality test. The results of this study indicated that there was no relationship between personality type and interface preference. There were also no performance differences between the two groups and no effect for personality type. In addition to this, an earlier review of studies that attempted to predict perform-ance from personality types (Koubek *et al.*, 1985) found that the correl-ations between personality and performance were weak.

However, there is research that suggests that personality does have an impact on the user's perception of the system they are interacting with. For example, Turkle (1984) found that users had a tendency to project personalities onto computer systems. I'm sure you've got annoyed at the 'stupid' computer when it loses the data that you failed to save or behaves in a way you did not expect. This idea of Turkle's has been developed most notably by the work of Reeves and Nash (1999). Reeves and Nash conducted a series of experiments whereby they asked people to rate the personality of the computer service they were inter-acting with (via text dialogue on a screen). Reeves and Nash found that by manipulating the dialogue on the screen, they could change people's perception of the personality of the system. In addition, they also found that people preferred interacting with a computer system whose personality was perceived by participants' to be similar to their own.

In relation to this it is also worth considering at this point, people's emotional responses to voice applications. This is especially true if one considers the voice applications that are currently offered by many mobile phone operators. For example, many of these companies con-duct market research into what type of voice they should have for the particular services in order to ensure that it conveys the proper image. In addition, one can also see the importance of personality when one considers location-based services which are on the way. In relation to this, I conducted a study with two colleagues (Love *et al.*, 2000) that investi-gated people's perception of the personality of a synthetic voice versus a pre-recorded voice (using the same female speaker in both conditions).

We found that the synthetic voice was perceived as having more negative personality traits such as being less agreeable and conscientious in comparison to the pre-recorded voice. One implication of these findings is that the voice you choose for an automated mobile phone service could have an impact on the uptake and continuing use of that system. For example, imagine you developed a speech-based automated tourist information guide service. You would want to make sure that your tourist guide service conveyed the 'proper' personality to the people who were using the service. In this case you would probably want the service to have personality traits such as extroversion (i.e. enthusiastically telling people about all the exciting things they can see and do in the city) and conscientiousness (i.e. telling people areas that they should avoid visiting in the city). However, on the other hand, if you were using a mobile phone banking service you may be put off by an assistant who told you in an extraverted tone that you were overdrawn on your account and had little prospect of getting an overdraft.

Another interesting dimension to personality and mobile phone use is that there also appears to be an emotional dimension to people's attitude towards their mobile phone. For example, Fortunanti (2001) puts forward the idea that people treat their mobile phone in an emotional way that is different to their attitude towards other types of technology, as they are regarded as being 'charismatic'. Thus people appear to be ascribing personality or anthropomorphic tendencies to their mobile phone.

So although the effect of personality on user performance when they are interacting with mobile ICTs may be weak, there is another aspect to this. Personality does appear to have an impact on people's attitudes and behaviour when using mobile devices in public places. An example of this can be seen with people's reaction to other people using mobile phones in restaurants, on the trains, etc. I will discuss this in greater detail in Chapter 6, which deals with an important issue for mobile devices: context of use. However, for the moment consider this: how would you describe the person who sits next to you in a crowded train and engages in a whole series of loud mobile phone conversations for the duration of your trip?

MEMORY

In psychology, researchers talk about people having long-term memory and something called working memory. Long-term memory is regarded as having unlimited capacity and we can hold information in our long term memory for long periods of time (although this ability often seems to desert us when it comes to sitting exams). On the other hand, working memory (or short-term memory as it used to be referred) has a limited capacity and we can only hold information in our working memory for a short period of time before it 'decays'.

The concept of working memory was developed by Baddeley and Hitch (1974) and Hitch and Baddeley (1976). They argued that the passive phrase 'short-term memory' should be replaced by the term 'working memory' as this aspect of memory is concerned with the active processing and temporary storage of visual and verbal information.

What affects could working memory have on an individual's ability to successfully use a mobile device or application? Well, when it comes to mobile applications such as speech-based mobile phone services, one can see the importance of taking into consideration the limitations of an individual's working memory. For example, when you are interacting with a speech-based mobile phone service (such as a cinema listings service) you have a single channel of serial information that cannot be scanned or browsed. As a user, you must try to remember the service structure, the menu options, and their location within the service hierarchy. This serial presentation of auditory information has been found to place great demands on working memory (Tun and Wingfield, 1997), especially in systems that have many menu options and levels. This point relates to what I said earlier in the section on spatial ability of the need for mobile application developers to reduce the complexity of the information they present to users in order to prevent problems of working memory overload and people feeling 'lost' whilst they are using the service or application.

VERBAL ABILITY

Language is ubiquitous, yet some individuals deal with verbal communications better than others. *Verbal ability* refers to the ability to comprehend spoken or written words, and can be measured using vocabulary and reading comprehension tests (such as the *AH Group Tests of General Intelligence*, Part 1, Heim, 1970). Verbal comprehension is a complex process which is composed of a number of sub-processes including lexical, syntactic, and pragmatic processes. What do these mean?

Lexical access: this is an automatic (unconscious) low level process which involves the matching of a string of words with stored templates that we have in long-term memory. Comprehension cannot proceed unless these tokens have been matched with their concepts.

Syntactic–semantic analysis: once words have been identified, the listener has to derive meaning. Syntactic rules identify the rules that each word plays in an expression. This is crucial to meaning. For example, syntax tells us that 'William likes Julie' is not the same as 'Julie likes William'. Semantic analysis enables the individual to decide the meaning of a word in context in an expression by combining the word's denotation with the specific role it has been assigned by a result of the syntactic analysis. 'William' in 'William likes Julie' and 'Julie likes William' has the same denotation, but in the first sentence it is the subject; in the second sentence it is what is known as the direct object. Basically, the contextual meaning of the word is different because of the different syntactic role of the name.

Pragmatic sub-process: this requires an individual to interpret the meaning of a message in terms of his or her understanding of what is happening. For example, 'Kenny saw the Campsie Hills flying to Glasgow'. The emphasis here is on context. If Kenny was watching a film with special effects he might well see the Campsie Hills flying to Glasgow. However, it would be more reasonable to assume that Kenny saw the Campsie Hills when he was in an aeroplane flying to Glasgow.

What happens now? Well these sub-processes appear to build upon one another: sentence analysis depends on lexical analysis and in turn, text comprehension depends on sentence comprehension.

What role does verbal ability play when people are interacting with ICTs? The results available for non-mobile environments suggest that verbal ability has not been found to consistently predict performance (Egan, 1988). In one of the few studies to find a conclusive effect of verbal ability, Vicente *et al.* (1987) found that verbal ability correlated significantly with a users' performance on their experimental task of searching for an item in a hierarchical file structure. With respect to automated phone services, Love *et al.* (1997) found that the performance of low verbal ability users was significantly poorer with a hierarchically structured automated music catalogue telephone service than high ability users, and it is perhaps not surprising that verbal ability is a stronger predictor of performance in speech-based systems than in visual interfaces. One can see the implications of this for speech-based mobile phone services which require the user to verbally comprehend the information provided in order to use the system effectively. It is not possible for the user to rely on a visual source of information, which means comprehension of the spoken prompts, messages and control options is of paramount importance.

PREVIOUS EXPERIENCE

In human–computer interaction research, previous experience has emerged as an important predictor of performance with a system (Egan, 1988). *Previous experience* refers to the user's experience with the actual interface used to perform a specific task; for example, navigating through a mobile phone voice mail service to get access to your stored messages. In contrast to this, domain knowledge refers to the knowledge and skill related to a task domain, for example, a proficient typist may transfer their skills to a computer text editing task. In relation to mobile HCI, it would be interesting to carry out an investigation into how well this skill transferred to using a detachable qwerty keyboard that comes with a PDA device or using the keyboard on a device such as a Blackberry. In HCI research, domain knowledge has generally been found to be a less important predictor of performance because such knowledge begins to benefit a user only after they have acquired experience of using a specific interface (Egan and Gomez, 1985).

Does this apply to mobile HCI too? Consider what happens if you change the brand and make of your mobile phone. You probably find that it takes you a bit of time to get used to interacting with your new device. For example, some mobile phone devices have a two-way navigational control keypad; some have a four-way directional keypad and others still use a roller wheel. In addition, do PDA devices offer a standardised format for interaction?

OLDER USERS

Have you ever seen an old person using a mobile phone in public or have you ever seen any adverts that try to appeal to older people to use their mobile phone? I've never seen the latter but I have seen older people using mobile phones in both private and public locations. Contrary to what you may think, older users (and here I'm talking about people who are over the age of 65) do use technology and yet their design needs often appear to have been overlooked by product designers. The aim of this section therefore is to look at issues related to the development of information communications technology products and services for the elderly.

Older users have a different set of user requirements from those of younger user groups, yet these needs do not appear to have been considered by product designers. However, the HCI community has a social and legal responsibility to this group of people. The numbers of older people in developing countries are growing and there is increasing evidence from surveys that indicate a growing trend for older people to become users of ICTs (ICM research for AgeConcern and Barclays, 2002). These surveys also found that 65 per cent of all those interviewed owned a mobile phone and used it regularly. In addition, in another survey of older users' usage of ICTs, Goodman *et al.* (2003) also found that a significant number of those interviewed in the 65–74 age group also owned a mobile phone (64%) and used it regularly. Yet there can be no doubt (as can be seen from the mobile phone marketing campaigns) that mobile phone services and handsets are designed with the 'typical' younger user in mind.

It would appear, judging from the results of these surveys, that those involved in ICT development are missing out on an important economic opportunity by failing to take into consideration the needs and priorities of this expanding group of people. Apart from the economic aspects of developing ICTs to meet the needs of elderly users, there is also the legal perspective to consider. In the United Kingdom, the Disability Discrimination Act (1995) requires organisations to ensure that any systems that they develop are accessible to people with disabilities. A similar piece of legislation exists in the USA in the shape of the Americans with Disabilities Act (ADA, 1990) which states that people should be able to use products and services on an equal basis.

Yet despite the economic opportunities, legal responsibilities, and research evidence that indicates that although this sector of the population is growing, older people are still often excluded in the design considerations of product designers in the technological sector (Czaja and Lee, 2003). Why is this the case? Keates and Clarkson (2002) suggest that some designers may find it easier to design products for younger people as they do not fully understand the different needs and priorities that older users have in comparison to their younger counterparts. This echoes what Cooper (1999) says when he refers to designers wittingly or unwittingly designing products for themselves in mind unless specifically told who to design for.

What are the needs and priorities of our older users? First of all, there are age-related impairments to consider. As we age, our mobile ability decreases (that is, our ability to move around as easily as we did when we were young, athletic undergraduates, declines). This may make it difficult for the older individual to move about the house and stretch up to the monitor to change the central heating settings, or it may be difficult to reach the telephone in the event of an emergency (such as after falling over in the garden). In addition, as we age, our hearing and vision starts to deteriorate too. What are the immediate implications of this? Firstly, in relation to vision, if your eyesight starts to deteriorate, it becomes increasingly difficult to read things like the newspaper and other forms of information when you are out in public places such as the library or at the train station. Now think about how difficult it would be for you to read the text on a PC screen or even on a mobile phone screen or a mobile device such as a PDA if your eyesight was not as good as it used to be. Secondly, in relation to hearing, for many older people their hearing ability can start to deteriorate and as a result of this, they could lose the ability to verbally communicate effectively with other people. This could have an effect on their ability to understand traditional information resources such as the train times. In addition to this, there is the memory aspect to consider. As people get older their memory can start to fail them. As a result of this, they may forget to do things like take essential medicines at specific times, or they may fail to remember where they have placed items in the house (such as their pension book) or if they have set their burglar alarm.

As well as these physical needs and priorities, many older users remain to be convinced about the benefits to them of using technology. This could be a reflection of what we said earlier on in this section about product design and marketing campaigns being aimed at the younger user. Yet, old people, as the results of the two surveys mentioned earlier demonstrate, do use ICTs and one of the key devices they use is the mobile phone.

Having looked at the physical characteristics of the older user, let's now turn our attention the research and designs issues involved when investigating the ICT needs and priorities of older users.

It's important in the HCI community that effective research and design methods are available to help developers make products and services that meet the needs and requirements of older users. These methods should provide information on: what specific functions they would like to see product or service providing (e.g. larger text on screen, larger buttons on handsets); why they would use a particular product; what kinds of technological developments would improve their quality of life both inside and outside the home.

So what kind of research has been carried out to date? There are very few pieces of research literature available that looks at older people in relation to mobile devices. Most of the work has focused on what is called 'smart home' technology (e.g. Lines and Hone, 2004) and older people's use of the internet in relation to interface design (e.g. Zajicek and Morrissey, 2001, Zajieck and Hall, 2000).

One key theme emerging from this research has been the importance of developing methodologies that allow both researchers and designers to get information on how to develop systems that meet the needs of older users. Gregor *et al.* (2002) argue that it is important to critically assess the methodology of design for older users as they have greater variability in physical, sensory and cognitive characteristics than younger users. In order to try and accommodate for the needs of the older user they propose the idea of a new design methodology called *user sensitive inclusive design*. This methodology should address issues such as:

- a greater variety of users' characteristics and functionality
- finding and recruiting representative users
- tailored, personalised and adaptive interfaces.

Could this design approach be effectively applied to investigate older people's use of mobile technology? Let's consider this question in a bit more detail.

Old people, like the rest of us, engage in activities outside the home and as we now know from the Age Concern and Barclays surveys, they have access to and use mobile technology. However, what are the implications of mobile device usage for older users? Well, like ICT development in general, mobile devices have not been designed with older users in mind. For example, the screens on mobile phones are small, as are the buttons on the keypads themselves. This may make it difficult for older users to see the information that is on the screen and interact with service via the keypad in an effective and satisfying way.

In addition, a lot of the terminology used for mobile devices (such as the desktop metaphor for PDA type devices) may seem like an alien concept to older users. There is also the *social* aspect of resistance to the uptake of new technology amongst older users. One social barrier facing designers is that many older users only see what Goodman *et al.* (2004) describe as the 'gimmiky' aspects of mobile devices.

But just think of the potential benefits that mobile devices could give older users: finding information about public transport (e.g. what time the bus is due), help for finding ones way about town, helping older people feel socially connected with friends and family, etc. Mobile devices could also be used to make them feel more secure. For example, they could use their mobile phone like a personal alarm (with a one key press speed dial option) should they get into difficulty in the home or even when they are outside. A mobile phone or a PDA device could also be used to control the functions of a smart home. For example, the individual could phone ahead to their house in order to activate the heating and lighting before they arrived home.

Ok, let's now look at a research example that adopted a user-sensitive inclusive design approach to mobile device development for older users. Goodman *et al.* (2004) conducted a study looking at a pedestrian navigation aid for an older group of adults. The aim of this study was to devise an aid that took into consideration their declining cognitive and motor skills (and perceptual skills). The device displayed landmarks (photographs appearing on the screen of a PDA type device) for users between their current location and where they were ultimately heading in order to help them get there. They found that the older age group enjoyed using it more than the younger age group who had also taken part in the study. In addition, when using the device as opposed to using a map, the older users got to their desired location a lot quicker. In contrast to this, younger users were slightly quicker getting to their desired location using a map rather than the mobile navigation device. What are the main implications from this study? Well it clearly shows that design choices that suit the needs and requirements of the older population may not be suitable for younger users. Therefore, there is the need for design methodologies that have this specific group of users in mind.

In general, what seems to be emerging from looking at the research on ICT development for the elderly is the need for a partnership between academic researchers, product and service developers in industry, and representative groups of users from the elderly community. This partnership should provide the framework to allow the development of design and research methodologies that result in the development of ICTs that meet the needs and requirements of the older user. In addition to this, it is clear that mobile devices, if properly developed, can make a significant positive contribution to improving the quality of life for the older user.

SUMMARY

It is a complex process to try and investigate and identify the effects of individual differences (such as age, personality and previous experience) on people's interaction with mobile technology and their attitude toward using mobile devices and applications. However, it is important for designers and product developers to realise that for most of the mobile devices and applications that they develop, the user population is heterogeneous.

Although most of the research to date has been carried out on non-mobile systems and applications, there is enough evidence to suggest that *individual* differences will be as equally important, if not more so, in the design of mobile applications. One key point that must be emphasised again here is the idea of universal access. It is vitally important that the needs of all user groups (e.g. the elderly and people with physical disabilities) are considered in the design process. This will be helped, of course, by more mobile HCI research that has particular focus on these user groups.

Another factor to consider is the idea of personalisation. Already we can see examples of individuals customising their mobile phones by choosing their own particular ring tone (and also having specific ring tones to identify different friends and relatives). Perhaps this concept will be developed in the future to allow people to adapt their mobile interface to reflect their needs and also to control and personalise the type of information services and entertainment services that they want to receive from their mobile provider.

Self test

- Spatial ability
- Verbal ability
- Working memory
- Psychometric test
- Personality traits
- Previous experience

Exercises

1. You have been asked to design a new location-aware mobile tourist information guide. What user characteristics will you accommodate for in you design?

2. Using a user sensitive inclusive design approach develop a user requirements gathering metric for a group of older users (age 65+) for a new mobile phone local bus timetable information service.

REFERENCES

Atkinson, R.L., Atkinson, R.C. and Hilgard, E.R. (1983) *Introduction to Psychology*, Harcourt Brace Janovich

Baddeley, A.D. and Hitch, G. (1974) Working memory. In *Recent Advances in Learning and Motivation*, Bower, G.A. (Ed.). Academic Press: New York

Chen, C., Czerwinski, M. and Macredie, R. (2000) Individual differences in virtual environments – introduction and overview. *Journal of the American Society for Information Science*, **51**(6), 499–507

Carroll, J.B. (1993) *Human Cognitive Abilities: a survey of factor-analytic studies*. Cambridge University Press, New York

Carver, C.S. and Scheier, M.F. (1992) *Perspectives on Personality*. Allyn and Bacon

Cooper, A. (1999) *The inmates are running the asylum*. SAMS Publishing, Indianapolis, IN

Czaja, S.J. and Lee, C.C. (2003) Designing for older adults. In *Human–Computer Interaction Handbook*, Jacko, J.A. and Sears, A. (Ed.), pp. 413–427, Mahaw, New Jersey

Egan, D. (1988) Individual differences in human–computer interaction. In *Handbook of Human–Computer Interaction*, Helander, M. (Ed.). Elsevier Science Publishers: North Holland, pp. 543–568

Egan, D.E. and Gomez, L.M. (1985) Assaying, isolating and accommodating individual differences in learning a complex skill. In *Individual Differences in Cognition*, Dillon, R.F. (Ed.). Academic Press: Orlando, pp. 173–217

Fortunanti, L. (2001) The mobile phone: an identity on the move, *Personal and Ubiquitous and Personal Computing*, **5**(2), 85–98

Goldberg, L.R. (1981) Language and individual differences: the search for universals in personality lexicons. In *Perspectives in Personality*, Carver, C.S. and Scheier, M.F. (Eds.). Allyn and Bacon

Goodman, J., Brewster, S. and Gray, P. (2004) Older people, mobile devices and navigation. *Proceedings of the Workshop on HCI and the Older Population*, Goodman, J. and Brewster, S. (Eds.), 7th September 2004 BCS HCI 2004, Leeds, UK

Goodman, J., Syme, A. and Eisma, R. (2003) Age-old question(naire)s. *Proceedings of Include 2003*, UK

Gregor, P., Newell, A. and Zajicek, M. (2002) Designing for dynamic diversity-interfaces for older people. In *Proceedings of the Fifth International ACM Conference on Assistive Technologies (ASSETS 2002)*, Edinburgh, UK, 8–10 July 2002

Heim, A.W. (1970) *AH4 Group Test of General Intelligence*, NFER, UK

Hitch, G. and Baddeley, A.D. (1976) Verbal reasoning and working memory, *Quarterly Journal of Experimental Psychology*, **28**, 603–621

ICM Research Survey (2002) www.icmresearch.co.uk/reviews/2002/it-internet-old-people.htm Accessed 12.01.05

Jung, C. (1971) *Psychological Types*. Kegan Paul Harcourt Brace and Co

Keates, S. and Clarkson, P.J. (2002) Defining design inclusion. In *Universal Access and Assistive Technology*, Keates, S. *et al.* (Eds.). Springer, Berlin, Heidelberg, New York

Koubek, R.J., LeBold, W.K. and Salvendy, G. (1985) Predicting performance in computer programming courses, *Behaviour and Information Technology*, **4**(2), 113–129

Lines, L. and Hone, K.S. (2004) Eliciting user requirements with older adults: lessons from the design of an interactive domestic alarm system. *Universal Access in the Information Society*, **3**(2), 141–148

Lohman, D.F. (1989) Human intelligence: an introduction to advances in theory and research, *Review of Educational Research*, **59**(4), 333–373

Love, S., Foster, J.C. and Jack, M.A. (1997) Assaying and isolating individual differences in automated telephone services, *Proceedings of the 16th International Conference on Human Factors in Telecommunications (HFT '97)*, pp. 323–330

Love, S., Foster, J.C. and Jack, M.A. (2000) Health warning: use of speech synthesis can cause personality changes. *State of the Art in Speech Synthesis*, pp. 14/1–14/8, IEE Publications, Savoy Place, London, UK

McCrae, R.R. and Costa, P.T. (1987) Validation of the five-factor model of personality across instruments and observers, *Journal of Personality and Social Psychology*, 52, 81–90

Morgan, K. and Macleod, H. (1990) The possible role of personality factors in computer interface preference. In *Second Interdisciplinary Workshop on Mental Models*, Robinson College, Cambridge

Reeves, B. and Nash, C. (1999) *The Media Equation: how people treat computers, television, and new media like real people and places.* Cambridge University Press, New York

Stanney, K. and Salvendy, G. (1995) Information visualisation: assisting low spatial individuals with information access tasks through the use of visual mediators, *Ergonomics*, **38**(6), 1184–1198

Tun, P.A. and Wingfield, A. (1997) Language and communication: fundamentals of speech communication and language processing in old age. In *Handbook of human factors and the older adult*, Fisk, A.D. and Rogers, W.A. (Eds.). Academic Press, San Diego

Turkle, S. (1984) *The Second Self: computers and the human spirit*. Granada Publishing

Vicente, K.J., Hayes, B.C. and Williges, R.C. (1988) Assaying and isolating individual differences in searching a hierarchical file system. *Human Factors*, **29**, 349–359

Vicente, K. and Williges, R. (1988) Accommodating individual differences in searching a hierarchical file system. *International Journal of Man-Machine Studies*, **29**, 647–668

Zajicek, M. and Brewster, S. (2004) A new research agenda for older adults. *Special Issue of Universal Access in the Information Society*. Volume 3, 2 June 2004

Zajicek, M. and Hall, S. (2000) Solutions for visually impaired people using the internet. *BCS HCI Sunderland 2000*, pp. 299–307

Zajicek, M. and Morrisey, W. (2001) Spoken message length for older adults. *Proceedings of INTERACT 2001*, pp. 789–790

SUGGESTED FURTHER READING

Carver, C.S. and Scheier, M.F. (2003) *Perspectives in Personality*, 5th edition. Allyn and Bacon

Eysenck, M. and Keane, M.T. (2000) *Cognitive Psychology: a student's handbook*, 4th edition. Psychology Press

3

Research methods

INTRODUCTION

This chapter focuses on looking at generic research methods relevant to human–computer interaction research, and used in user centered information systems design and development. It should be pointed out that this is intended to be essentially an introduction to the types of methods that can be particularly useful in relation to mobile HCI research and not an in-depth look at all the techniques available. The references and further reading lists at the end of the chapter direct you to texts where you will be able to find out more information on quantitative and qualitative methods. It should also be mentioned that there can be overlaps between the tools and techniques used in each of the research methods approaches that will be discussed in this chapter.

SETTINGS FOR YOUR STUDY

There are basically two types of settings you can use to conduct your mobile HCI research study: in the laboratory or in a field setting. The latter may not actually take place in a field, but your study could take place in the actual environment in which people are using the mobile technology. Let us take, as an example, an employee of a gas company as he goes about his calls using a PDA device to log the problems and the work carried out at each house visited. To begin with, let's look at the laboratory setting.

Laboratory settings

This has been the traditional approach to HCI methods research. In this case, you would get people coming into the lab to take part in a study. In this set-up you would control the environment in order to test your specific hypotheses. This would allow you to see how they react to using a new piece of mobile technology without anything distracting them from the task in hand. For example, you may be interested in developing a synthetic speech interface for a cinema listings service. One key aspect of this could be to find out what is the minimum level of recognition accuracy (on the part of your service) that users are willing to accept. In order to investigate this you may test participants in your study with three different versions of recognition accuracy. After each version of the service you could ask participants what they thought of that service and at the end of the study you would have information on what service they liked the best.

Field experiment

A field experiment obviously does not give you control over all your variables and settings in the same way as a laboratory experiment does. However, it can be a very effective form of research method for mobile HCI research. The reason for this is that mobile devices and applications are used in dynamic social environments (e.g. in a café, on the train). Therefore, it is important for researchers (and designers) to assess how context of use affects people's performance and attitude towards using mobile devices and applications. However, one similarity between the field experiment and the lab-based experiment is that elements of the study can still be controlled by the experimenter; for example, asking participants in your study to use a speech-interface version of a location-based mobile phone tourist information service and comparing it with their attitudes and performance with a key pad interface version of the same service. In this study, you may find that participants find it difficult to use speech input when they are in a noisy street, as the service misunderstands what they are saying and provides the user with information they did not ask for.

EXPERIMENTAL VARIABLES

There are two types of variables used in an experiment: the *dependent variable* and the *independent variable*. The independent variable is usually manipulated in some way in an experiment. For example, in a mobile HCI context, you may be interested in looking at the effects of two different types of navigation styles for a mobile phone service; speech and touch-tone on a group of participants' attitude towards the usability of the service. In this instance, the type of service style (i.e. speech or touch-tone) would be classed as the independent variable. On the other hand, the dependent variable is so called because it is dependent on the independent variable. Dependent variables are the *outcomes caused* by the independent variable. In our example of the two types of mobile phone interaction styles, what do you think the dependent variable would be? One dependent variable could be participants' attitudes towards the usability of the mobile phone service as it is dependent on the style of interaction that is being used.

However, you should be aware that you can have more that one independent variable in an experiment. For example, you may be interested in looking at mode of input (i.e. speech or touch-tone) and menu style (hierarchical, relational). In addition, it goes without saying that you can also have more than one dependent variable in an experiment. For example, two dependent variables you could have for the study mentioned above are: users' attitudes towards the usability of the service, and the time taken by participants to complete the same tasks using the two different versions of the service.

EXPERIMENTAL DESIGNS

If you are interested in carrying out an experimental study as part of your research into a specific aspect of mobile HCI, it is important to understand the different types of experimental design that are available to you. This will help you to design an experiment that should help you meet the aims and objectives of your study. Therefore, what follows below is an introduction to the different types of experimental design you can use in your mobile HCI research work.

Repeated measures design

The repeated measures experimental design is part of a group of designs known as related designs (the other main type being matched-pairs design). These are also known as *within-groups designs*. In a repeated measures design you can use one group of participants and test them in both experimental conditions. In the example we have been using throughout this chapter so far, that would be getting participants to use both the speech interface and the touch-tone interface for the new mobile phone service. In this case, there is no control group because participants are the same in both conditions. Therefore, the participants act as their own control group because any difference in results for the two conditions can't be put down to the people being different from one another but must be due, in part, to the independent variable that is being manipulated. For example, people may find information quicker using the key pad version of the service in comparison to the time it takes them to find similar information using the speech version of the same service. One of the possible disadvantages of using this experimental design is the possibility of order effects occurring. 'What are order effects', I hear you ask. Order effects can be the result of people improving through practice. Therefore, if they are being asked to use two new navigational techniques for a location aware mobile device, it would be hard to see which one is better if participants always do version A followed by version B. There may also be a practice factor to consider. For example, it may take half an hour to complete all the tasks associated with version A, so that by the time people are half-way through using system B they are becoming better through practice or getting tired (this is known as a *fatigue effect*).

However, do not worry too much – there are various ways of getting round order effects. As a general rule of thumb you should counter-balance (or randomise) the order of experimental conditions so that one person gets version A followed by version B and another person gets version B followed by version A. If it does take a relatively long time for participants to complete all the tasks associated with version A, you should give participants a break and if your research budget allows it, offer them some tea, coffee, soft drinks and biscuits. It will work wonders for their morale!

Independent samples design

As the name suggests, in an independent samples design different people take part in each condition. So in our experiment we would have to find one group of people to use the speech-input version of the mobile phone service and another group of people to use the touch-tone version of the service. However, they would still be measured using the same dependent variables. There are advantages to using this type of experimental design such as there will be no order effects or worries about participants getting fatigued during the experiment. The disadvantages of using this approach are that you do not have control over participant variables (this means individual differences such as age, gender, experience of using mobile applications that could have a significant effect on people's performance in your study) and you need to find two groups of people to take part in your study. This could be costly and time-consuming, especially if you are working to short timescales.

Matched-pairs design

A matched-pair design is known as a related design because the groups of participants who take part in your study have been 'matched' on certain criteria. For example, say you wanted to compare people's attitudes towards a speech input device for a mobile phone service and a touch-tone version of the same service. People could be matched in terms of age, gender and experience is using mobile phone information services such as the one you are testing.

The advantages of using a matched-pairs design approach is that there are no order effects, and you are still controlling some of the participant variables (e.g. age, gender). The disadvantages of using this method are that there could be some participant characteristics that are present that could have a confounding effect on your results. For example, imagine the first group of volunteers were paid for participating in your study and the second group was not, what kind of affect do you think that could have on the responses they give?

EXTERNAL AND INTERNAL VALIDITY

From the example we have given through this chapter so far, we are interested in looking at the affects of the independent variable (speech input system versus a touch-tone system for a mobile information service) on the dependent variable (people's perception of usability of the mobile information service). Now say you show the results to a friend and she says 'ah, but perhaps some of the participants were biased against speech from the start, that's why touch-tone came out better'. Although you may be tempted at this point to downgrade your friend's status to that of an associate you occasionally speak to, they have in fact highlighted an important issue that you should be aware of. Do the results of your study really have any internal and external validity?

Internal validity is concerned with factors within the study itself that could be leading you to wrongly interpret your results in favour of the initial hypothesis you came up with. For example, order effects or bias in the groups (yes, you realise now that the majority of people in the speech-interface group were in fact from the 'speech-based mobile phones applications are rubbish and should never be used in public places' action group).

External validity, as the term suggests, is concerned with whether or not you can generalise the findings from your study to the way the population at large would behave, or in this case feel, towards using a speech-based mobile information service. Would people using the speech-based service feel the same way towards it if they were using it in different places (e.g. in the street, sitting in a café)?. This is known as *ecological validity*. One way to try and address this problem, would be to carry out a follow-up study on a larger sample, drawn from another group of people from the general public, and compare the results from this study with the results obtained from the first study.

HYPOTHESES TESTING

A hypothesis can be described as a concise prediction about the outcome of an experiment. For example, you could predict that a group of participants will prefer a speech-based version of a mobile information service to a touch-tone version of the system. This would be called a *one-tailed* hypothesis as you are specifically stating which version of the service will be preferred over the other. On the other hand, you could say that participants will have a preference for either the speech-based mobile phone service or the touch-tone version of the service. As you are not predicting which version participants will prefer, this is known as a *two-tailed* hypothesis. The aim of all experiments is to reject the *null-hypothesis*. This is also known as the alternative hypothesis. The null-hypothesis states that there would be no difference in user preference for the two versions of the mobile phone information service. Any differences that you do find are due to chance, and have nothing to do with the independent variable you are manipulating.

SAMPLING TECHNIQUES

A group of people selected from the general population to take part in your experiment are known as a *sample*. Not surprisingly, there are various ways to select your sample based on the aims of the experiment or study you are conducting. There are different types of sampling techniques at your disposal. Here are some of the main ones that you should be aware of.

Biased sample

Remember what we were saying earlier about the results of your study having external and internal validity? We need to be sure that the sample of people who take part in our study are representative of the population at large or we could have problems with external validity, i.e. our sample is biased. For example, say you want to test the perceived usability of a new speech-based mobile phone information service. How would you go about choosing participants to take part in your study? How representative of the population at large would they be if you chose your sample from a second-year undergraduate Psychology class? You should try and match your participants as closely as possible to the target group your new service will be aimed at. So how do you go about trying to get a more representative group?

Random samples

If we are not interested in a specific type of person (e.g. the attitudes of 15-year-olds to a new downloaded music service available on their mobile phones) then a random sample is the only way to get a representative sample of the general population. This would certainly be the case if you wanted to find out the general public's attitude towards mobile phone use in public places.

A truly random sample does not mean grabbing people in the student union canteen and asking them to complete your questionnaire. Nor does it mean grabbing people's names from the phone book. It is often hard as a student to get a truly random sample of people, but you should always strive to have a representative group of the population as a whole to take part in your study.

How can you get a truly random sample? Well, some would say that it is not possible to get a truly random sample in practice. Therefore, researchers usually concentrate on one of the following techniques.

Stratified sampling

The aim of this type of sampling is to get a specific number of people in your experimental sample that actually reflects your target population. Say for example, a very generous mobile phone company has decided to provide students on your campus with a free mobile phone as part of a study looking at students getting access to university information as they walk about the campus. In order to get a stratified sample of students you would have to do something like this:

If 10 per cent of students on the campus were information systems and computing science students, then 10 per cent of your sample population should be made up from students on those courses. In terms of actual numbers, if your whole sample size is going to be 200 students then 20 of these students have to come from the information systems and computing courses.

Quota sampling

This type of sampling technique is one that you may be more familiar with as it's the kind often used by market research companies. Yes, you've seen those people making a bee-line for you sometimes as you walk down the street. So why me? You may ask.

The reason the street interviewer may stop you is because they have to get four female and four male students aged between 18 and 20 in order to ask them questions about a new type of mobile phone service. The idea behind quota sampling is that the interviewer would stop interviewing students who fell into this category or strata of the population once their target quota had been reached.

Cluster samples

Here's an example that explains the principle behind cluster sampling. Imagine you are interested in investigating the possibility of using broadband technology to provide local information services via a mobile phone. In order to carry out this study, it makes sense to go where there is a clustering of broadband users. For example, this could be a street or a specific geographical location within a town. By adopting this approach you can potentially save time and effort on recruiting suitable participants for your study.

Opportunity samples

As an undergraduate student carrying out a final-year project looking at navigational devices for a new 3g mobile phone service, this could be the most easily available sampling technique available to you. As the name suggests, opportunity sampling is based on the idea of choosing the people who are the most easily available to you, at that time, for testing your navigational design. However, if you do go down this road you should be aware of the pitfalls that were mentioned earlier in relation to external and internal validity as well as sampling bias.

SAMPLE SIZE

This is an area of debate within the HCI community. Some well-known usability experts such as Jakob Neilson (1993) argue that you can get the main results in a usability evaluation exercise (i.e. highlighting the main problem with an interface) by using between five and ten participants. However, if you read other research methods books by people such as Coolican (2000) you will note that they argue that in order to investigate the effects of an experimental independent variable (remember our example of people comparing a speech and touch-tone version of mobile phone information service), the ideal number of participants to have is about 30. This figure is considered to be large enough to highlight *true* (i.e. not chance) experimental differences using experimental techniques. If you don't find any significant difference in users attitudes towards the two versions of the service with a sample of this size, you still have to try and find answers for the results you obtained. For example, it may be that the task did not challenge the participants enough to allow them to make a comparison between the relative merits of speech as opposed to touch-tone. Or, it could be down to the fact that the participants were all very mobile friendly and would be quite happy to use either (or a combination of both) versions of the service.

DATA COLLECTION METHODS

This section of the chapter will focus on different ways that you collect data for your study. Some of these are used in various fields of study (e.g. questionnaires), whereas others are more specific to the area of HCI (e.g. cognitive walkthrough) and are discussed in the next chapter.

Questionnaire design

This is a common tool used for gathering data in the area of HCI. A questionnaire is a good way of getting information from a participant on their attitudes towards a service they are using (e.g. speech versus touch-tone). It can also be used as part of the design process, such as the requirements gathering stage. You can also use a questionnaire to obtain factual information from participants in relation to their experience of using particular types of technology. This information could then be used, for example, as an independent variable in your study (e.g. own a mobile phone/do not own a mobile phone).

Scaler questionnaires

One of the most popular types of questionnaire designs used in HCI is the scaler questionnaire. An example of what I mean by a scaler question-naire is shown in Figure 3.1. This could be the kind of questionnaire

1. The automated cinema information service was easy to use

| Strongly Agree | Agree | Neutral | Disagree | Strongly Disagree |

2. I sometimes felt lost when using the automated cinema information service

| Strongly Agree | Agree | Neutral | Disagree | Strongly Disagree |

3. I would be happy to use the automated cinema information service again

| Strongly Agree | Agree | Neutral | Disagree | Strongly Disagree |

4. I thought the automated cinema information service was polite

| Strongly Agree | Agree | Neutral | Disagree | Strongly Disagree |

Figure 3.1   Example of a Scaler Questionnaire

you would get participants to complete in order to find out their attitude towards an automated cinema listing service provided by a mobile phone operator.

Figure 3.1 is an example of a scaler questionnaire known as a Likert questionnaire (Likert, 1932). As can be seen from the example, with this kind of questionnaire the participant is asked to indicate the extent to which they agree or disagree with a particular statement. The idea is to generate a group of statements like the ones in our example and then to add up a participant's response to each statement to give an overall score for an individual participant. This score could reflect their attitude towards the usability of the service or system being considered in your study.

If you want to know more on how to construct a Likert-type usability questionnaire please refer to Technical Tip 1.

Technical Tip 1

Constructing a Likert-Type Usability Questionnaire

1. The first thing you have to do when constructing a usability question-naire is to think about the statements you want to have in it. You need to make sure that you know what it is you are looking for. For example, what aspects of the usability of the system are you interested in find-ing out about? Is it the attitude towards the voice you have used; is it how people find navigating around the menu structures to get to the information that they are looking for? If in doubt, go back and look at the aims and objectives of your study to help you generate relevant statements.

2. In constructing your Likert questionnaire it is important that you try to have an equal number of positively worded statements and negatively worded statements. This is important in order to control for the '*acquiescence effect*'. This is a phenomenon whereby participants in a study may unwittingly try to respond positively to every question in order to help the investigator with their study. Or alternatively, they may respond negatively to every question if they don't like you!

3. The next step is to collect data from participants by getting them to complete the questionnaire.

4. After that, the next stage is to score participants' responses to your statements. If it is a positively worded statement you may scale responses as shown in Figure 3.2.

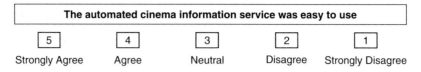

The automated cinema information service was easy to use

5	4	3	2	1
Strongly Agree	Agree	Neutral	Disagree	Strongly Disagree

Figure 3.2   Scoring for positively worded statements in a Likert-type questionnaire

I felt lost while using the automated cinema service

1	2	3	4	5
Strongly Agree	Agree	Neutral	Disagree	Strongly Disagree

Figure 3.3   Scoring for negatively worded statements in a Likert-type questionnaire

Therefore, if the person responds to this statement by ticking the strongly agree box you would give them a score of 5 for this statement. This suggests a strong positive attitude to this statement. However, when it comes to scoring negatively worded statements the idea is to *reverse the polarity* of your scoring system. An example of the scoring system you would employ for negatively worded statements is shown in Figure 3.3.

In this case, if the person strongly agrees with the statement, they would receive a score of 1. This suggests a strong negative attitude towards the navigational aspects of interacting with the service. However, if they did not agree with this statement and didn't feel lost, they would tick the strongly disagree box and obtain a score of 5.

5. As you will see from the above examples (hopefully!) the person should be forced to think about what they are answering rather than blindly ticking 'strongly agree' to every statement on the scale. In addition, it is important to mix-up the presentation of your positive and negatively worded statements in your Likert scale in order to minimise the risk of what is known as *constant error* caused by the acquiescence effect.

6. The next step is to enter your scores into a data spreadsheet (see Figure 3.4).

From this spreadsheet you could calculate each participant's overall usability by adding up their scores in question 1 to question 4. In addition, you could get an overall usability score for each question by adding up all the scores in each of the question columns. Once you have this type of data you could then look, for example, at differences in usability scores between sub-sets of your participants (i.e. different

Participant	Question 1	Question 2	Question 3	Question 4
1	5	4	5	5
2	3	1	4	2
3	4	3	3	2
4	4	4	5	4
5	5	5	4	5

Figure 3.4   Data spreadsheet for entering participants' scores

age groups or differences between males and females) or you could look at the total scores for each question to identify any weaknesses the system may have. Of course, as you know, the type of analysis that you undertake should be driven by the aims and objectives of your study.

Semantic differential scale

Another type of scaler questionnaire is the *semantic differential scale* (Osgood *et al.*, 1957). In a semantic differential scale an individual has to place a mark on scale between two bipolar adjectives based on how they feel towards the object. For example, imagine you have developed a speech-based mobile phone information service and you are interested in what people thought about the voice. An example of the semantic differential scale you develop to assess this is shown in Figure 3.5.

As with the Likert-type questionnaire, you would ask participants to complete this after they had used the speech-based mobile phone service and answer these statements in relation to the voice that they

Friendly	---	---	---	---	---	---	---	Unfriendly
Polite	---	---	---	---	---	---	---	Impolite
Happy	---	---	---	---	---	---	---	Sad
Loud	---	---	---	---	---	---	---	Quiet
Easy to understand	---	---	---	---	---	---	---	Difficult to understand
Trustworthy	---	---	---	---	---	---	---	Unreliable

Figure 3.5   Example of the semantic differential scale

Easy to understand	---	---	---	---	---	-x-	---	Difficult to understand
	7	6	5	4	3	2	1	
Trustworthy	---	-x-	---	---	---	---	---	Unreliable
	7	6	5	4	3	2	1	

Figure 3.6   Recording a participant's understanding of mobile phone use

had just heard. Once again, each 'tick' that a person enters would be converted into a score by you before you input the data into a spreadsheet or the like for analysis. The scoring system is similar to the one used for the Likert example that we mentioned earlier: the higher the score the more positive that particular object was perceived by the participant. Therefore, using the example shown in Figure 3.6, if the participant perceives the voice as being difficult to understand, this would be seen as a negative response and would receive a score of 2. Whereas if they felt the voice was trustworthy, it would receive a score of 6, as this is regarded as a positive response.

Once you have scored each participant's responses you would then input them into a data spreadsheet to allow you to carry out a formal data analysis.

Issues to be aware of in scaler questionnaire design

In relation to the types of questionnaire designs that I have just described, there are a few issues you should be aware of. One problem that both the Likert scale and the semantic differential scale have is the problem of the mid-point on the scale. Does it really mean that the user is neutral when they choose this option or are they really not sure which direction they would rather go in?

Another factor that you should consider when constructing these types of scale, is how discriminating are the items that you have chosen to make up your scale? Discrimination refers to questions (or statements) which differentiate between high and low scorers on your scale. If all of the participants in your study respond in the same way to a question (e.g. give it a score of 7), then the question (or statement) is regarded as not discriminating between users, and therefore should be excluded. In addition, you should make sure that you are not asking questions that are too similar in your questionnaire. For example, if you have a statement that said '*I enjoyed using the automated cinema list-ing service*' you would not want to include another statement such as '*the automated cinema listing service was entertaining to use*'. Why? Because these two questions are basically the same, they both want to know how enjoyable you found the experience of using the automated cinema listing service. There are a number of ways you could deal with the problem of including statements that are too similar. One approach could be to get a friend or colleague to go through your questionnaire to weed out any inappropriate statements. You could even ask your project supervisor to do this, but remember to give them enough time (i.e. not the day before you start your evaluation) to give you feedback on this. A more formal approach would be to undertake a statistical technique known as *item analysis*. This basically requires you to give a group of participants your questionnaire to complete (bear in mind that this may require them to use the system or service that you will formally assess at a later stage). Once you have this data, the idea behind item analysis is that you compare the score for each individual statement against the overall usability score you obtained from your question-naire. The following steps should then be undertaken:

1. work out the correlation for each item (e.g. each individual state-ment score) and the total score for the questionnaire
2. only keep those items in your questionnaire which correlate highly with the overall scale score
3. items which do not correlate highly with the overall scale score are measuring something different from what you think they are measuring.

For a fuller discussion of this topic I suggest you look at Coolican (2000).

One last thing you need to think about is the actual length of your questionnaire. I suggest that you keep your final version down to a maximum of about 20 statements. Remember that it is time-consuming for people (not to mention testing their patience) to complete these, especially if they have already spent half an hour actually using your system or service.

PERFORMANCE MEASURES

This section will focus on the types of performance measures that you can use to help you collect data as part of your mobile HCI study.

Traditionally in HCI research performance measures often make use of methods and techniques borrowed from experimental psychology.

Task completion times

How long it takes a person to complete a specific task you have set them can be used as a performance measure for the mobile technology you are testing. This is a standard performance measure that is used in most areas of HCI research. For example, when evaluating an automated cinema listing service, accessed using a mobile phone, you could give participants in your study specific tasks to complete as part of your comparison of speech versus key pad input for this service. One way you could approach this is to sit with a stopwatch and time participants from the start to finish of each task. In this case, you would have to be sure that you know when the person has finished each task. You could, for example, simply ask them to tell you when they have finished each task. However, one thing you need to be aware of is that speed of performance does not necessarily tell you how difficult the users found the task. Therefore, you should always include a range of performance measures in your study.

Errors

The mistakes that people make when trying to complete the tasks you have set them are also a good measure of performance. For example, if people continually get lost when they are looking for information on parking facilities using the automated cinema listing service, this could be an indication that there are problems with the path they have to take through the service to get to this information. Errors can be recorded in a number of ways. One method would be to sit and observe people interacting with the service and record the number and the nature of errors as they occur. Another approach would be to automate the process if at all possible by creating a log file that records all the data input from the user in the course of a trial. Afterwards you would go through the file noting the number and types of errors for each participant in your study.

Interrupts

This performance measure is usually only applicable to speech-based mobile applications. When we interact with an automated (or synthetic speech) service we interact with the service by responding to dialogue prompts that the system provides for us. For example, in our automated cinema listing we may hear the following prompt from the service '*Welcome to the automated cinema listing service. For films currently showing press 1; for details on how to book tickets press 2; for informa- tion on how to get here press 3; for general information press 4*'. The idea is that we choose the option we want by pressing the appropriate num- ber on the key pad or verbally saying the option number that we want. We would then continue our interactions with the service in this manner until we had completed the task that we wanted to undertake.

Now, if you are a frequent user of this service or hear the option you want at the start of the list, you may interrupt the prompt from the ser- vice and input you preferred option number. It is the number of inter- ruptions to prompts from the service that form the basis of the interrupt rates that you can use as a measure of performance. Interrupt rate can be defined as the number of times that a user keyed in (or uttered a response) before the end of a prompt by the system divided by the overall number of responses made by a user to menu prompts from the service throughout the trial.

In one study I carried out looking at age differences when people were using a speech-based automated music catalogue service (Love *et al.*, 1997), I found out that the reason older people failed to interrupt the service as often as younger users had nothing to do with navigational problems or understanding the prompts. In fact, the older people thought it was rude to interrupt the service while it was speaking.

Silences

As with interrupt rates, silence rates are usually only measured when people are interacting with a speech-based service. When mobile phone operators are designing the dialogues for their services, they start working on the principle that after the service delivers a prompt to a user, the user has about 5 seconds to make a response. If they fail to respond within 5 seconds (or the specific time period that the dialogue designers have specified) this is known as a *time out* and the system will prompt the user again for a response. Silence rate can therefore be defined as the number of times a user did not respond by the end of a timeout period following a system prompt divided by the overall num- ber of responses made by a user to menu prompts from the service throughout the trial. One way you could record silences would be to listen to the system and the user's response, using a set of headphones.

This can be quite a sophisticated form of measurement to obtain and you may need to employ a Wizard of OZ set-up (which we discuss in Chapter 6) to allow you to use this as a performance measure.

Retention

Strictly speaking, this is not a measure of performance but a technique used in measuring performance over time. This is an approach whereby you could obtain data on the measures of performance that we have listed above over a period of time. This is an important point to consider as people may perform differently, based on the amount of mobile application experience they have had; this is the point where you may hear people talk about users becoming *habituated* to a service or system. Essentially, this implies that they know how to use a service and interact with it successfully.

For example, you could carry out your study over a four-week period and arrange to contact your participants, on their mobile phone, at a certain time each week and ask them to complete a series of tasks using the automated cinema listing guide. You could collect performance data using monitoring software such as TrueActive (TrueActive Corporation, Kennewick, WA) to log the sound files that participants used. This would allow you to compare performance results over the study period. You could also carry out interviews each week after participants had completed their tasks to investigate if their attitude towards the service had changed over a period of time. Taken all together, this data could provide you with useful information on the way people used the system and if some parts of the system (such as specific navigation cues) were easier to remember than others.

Observation

In an observational study, the emphasis is on observing the naturally occurring behaviour of people (with or without them knowing about it). In an HCI context, observational techniques have been used as part of the data collection process in the lab. For example, you can watch people's reactions as they interact with a new PDA interface, observing where they have difficulties or which parts of the interface they do not like. This would be classed as *controlled observation* as the users are in a controlled lab environment. Observational techniques are also a very useful form of data collection for mobile HCI studies. For example, they have been widely used in studies where the emphasis is on investigating people's reaction to mobile phone use in public places (e.g. Ling, 2002). This would be classed as *naturalistic observation* as you are observing the behaviour as it naturally occurs in its normal context of use. Now let's have a look at the different techniques that you can use to collect data in an observational study.

Audiotape recording

This is your own verbal record (recorded onto audiotape) of the behaviour of the people you are observing as it occurs. If you decide on this approach in the lab you would have to make sure that your recording was unobtrusive and did not distract users from carrying out the tasks that you had asked them to do. However, how useful would it be to try and record your observations on to an audiotape when you were observing people's reaction to mobile phone use in public places? You may find that you could start to draw attention to yourself, with people becoming uneasy about you looking at them while you are speaking into a small tape recorder at the same time.

Videotape recording

This could provide you with a very rich source of data. For example, you can record people's reactions to the initial intrusion of a mobile phone ringing next to them in a café and then watch their subsequent reactions for the duration of the call (and afterwards too!). However, you may have problems with maintaining your 'covert' status. How would you feel if you saw some strange guy pointing a camcorder at you as you were explaining to your friend how irritated you were becoming about the guy sitting next to you in the restaurant using his mobile phone all the time? Also, in a situation like this you would need to ask the restaurant owner first before you started filming. In addition, there is a time factor to consider here – it may take a long time for you to record an adequate sample of 'events' for your study; or you may not have allocated enough time in your project plan to capture all the data you need.

Coding form

This is a very good option if you can't get away with using a video recorder. The danger in trying to write down what you observe is that you may try and write everything down that you see and in the process of trying to do this, miss some crucial social behaviour or interaction. So what's the solution? It's developing your own coding form. This should be used, ideally, after you have collected some initial data and piloted your coding system. This is time-consuming but very worthwhile. Let's look at how you would go about this in more detail by looking at Technical Tip 2.

Technical Tip 2

Constructing an observational coding form

1. The first thing you have to do is to be clear about what it is you are interested in observing. For the purposes of this example, we are interested in looking at an individual's behaviour when they are sitting next to a stranger who makes or receives a mobile phone call in a public place such as a waiting room.
2. Next, identify what you think are the dimensions or categories of behaviour that you expect to observe. In this instance, you could have three categories and you could design your coding form as shown in Figure 3.7.
3. Once you have designed this initial form, test it out in a waiting room to see if it is covering the main behaviours that you have highlighted. This process will also allow you to add new behaviour categories that you had not previously thought of.
4. Another way to test the reliability of your coding form is to get a few of your friends to use it (if you persuade them to help you) and record their observations and see how it compares with your own. Obviously you would all have to observe the same social scene to do this, at the same time.
5. Next, it's time for you to collect your data for real. At this stage, you will choose a waiting room and start your observational study. Remember, depending on the place you decide to conduct your study, you may have to get permission first before you start.
6. You should also be aware that it may take you a few days (or perhaps even longer) to collect the observational data that you need for your study. Make sure then, that you allocate enough time to do this in your project plan.

Pre-mobile phone call behaviour	
The two people acknowledge each other before the phone call	Yes/No
They speak to each other	Yes/No
How often?	
They sit in silence	Yes/No
They pick up reading materials after initially acknowledging each other	Yes/No
Other behaviours observed	
Additional Comments	

Behaviour during the mobile phone call	
The person receiving the call turns away from the person sitting next to them	Yes/No
The bystander to the mobile phone call averts their gaze from the person receiving the call	Yes/No
The person receiving the call lowers their voice when speaking	Yes/No
The bystander to the mobile phone call turns their body away from the person receiving the mobile phone call	Yes/No
The bystander picks up reading material and starts to read it	Yes/No
The bystander sits and stares straight ahead	Yes/No
The bystander glances at the person on the mobile phone	Yes/No
How often?	
The bystander gets up and walks over to another part of the waiting room and sits down	Yes/No
The bystander looks at their watch	Yes/No
How often?	
The person receiving the mobile phone call gets up and moves to another part of the waiting room	Yes/No
Other Observations	
Additional Comments	

Post-mobile phone call behaviour	
The bystander smiles at the receiver of the mobile phone call as it finishes	Yes/No
The person who received the mobile phone call apologises to the bystander	Yes/No
The bystander comes back to sit in their original seat (if they moved)	Yes/No
The receiver of the mobile phone call comes back to sit in their original seat (if they moved)	Yes/No
The two people start to talk again	Yes/No
Other Observations	
Additional Comments	

Figure 3.7 Example of a Coding Form

7. Once you have collected the data, you can transfer it from the coding sheets into a spreadsheet for statistical analysis. I would use the same category headings in the spreadsheet that you used in the coding form. For example, you could provide frequency scores for specific behaviours that were observed. You could also look for differences in behaviour between males and females, and different age groups.

Before you undertake any observational studies you should ask yourself if there are any ethical considerations you should be aware of. For example, the idea of 'unobtrusive' observation is that you can observe the behaviour of the people in as 'natural' a way as possible, thus reducing the risk of contaminating your data by people unwittingly taking part in your research. However, this raises the issue of informed consent. The main problem here is how you get people to consent to participate in your study as they are actually there and carrying out the activity you are interested in anyway. For guidance on this matter you should consult the ethical guidelines of a professional body, such as the British Psychological Society, The British Computer Society, The Association for Computing Machinery, and the like. You should even go and talk this over with one of your college tutors too.

INTERVIEWS

Questioning an individual can be a quick way of getting information from them on usability issues, requirements gathering and a whole host of mobile HCI research interests. An interview can be used in the lab at the end of a formal testing session to help find out some more information on what participants thought about the experiment that they had just taken part in. It can also be used to investigate how participants' interview answers compare to their behaviour which you will have observed during the experiment and also, the performance data that you may have logged during the experiment (e.g. timings for completing each task you asked them to undertake as part of the study). Interviews come in various formats and the following are probably the most commonly used in HCI to illicit information from participants.

Informal interviews

This type of interview is totally unstructured with the aim of the interview being to try and collect as much data as possible. It would probably be a good idea to ask participants if you could record their responses in this type of situation, just in case your writing speed isn't quite as fast as you thought it was (you don't want to miss out on any crucial insights that participants give you, do you?).

Semi-formal interview

This type of interview would work well after you have had a chance to look at the data you have already collected from participants in a lab session. For example, you may have noticed that nearly all participants had problems following a particular series of links to find information. Does this suggest that the links are badly named or is it more to do with spatial navigational difficulties? Essentially, you would use this type of interview to cover a set of topics that your initial analysis and observations of the lab performance have brought to light. There is no set order to the discussion of these topics and you can 'go with the flow' as they say. However, you should make sure that you cover all the topics that you are interested in and also follow up any new avenues which may have opened up by this type of discussion. This approach is similar, in some ways, to the approach that is often adopted in focus groups. A focus group, in this instance, is where you bring together a group of participants, who will have taken part in your study in order to find out some more information on specific issues (e.g. specific problems people had with some of the navigational cues) that you observed in the course of the study or that emerged from some preliminary data analysis that you carried out.

You can also use this form of interview in context, immediately after a user has completed the tasks that you asked them to undertake. This is known as *retrospective analysis*. In this instance you could play back a recording of the participant's session and ask them to explain in a bit more detail why they were having problems at the specific points when using the service that you highlight.

Semi-structured interview

In a semi-structured interview you have a set number of questions which are presented in the same order. These types of questions could come at the end of a Likert-type questionnaire that you have asked participants to complete in order to assess their perception of the usability of a new mobile phone service, such as *'is there anything you particularly liked about the service?'; 'have you any other comments that you would like to make?'.*

An important thing to remember when you are using open-ended questions is to phrase them so as to encourage participants to give as much information as possible. You would also want to find out *why* participants would or would not use the service again. Therefore, when using this type of questioning you should be prepared to prompt participants gently with follow-up questions, using stock phrases such as *'could you expand on that please?'* or *'why would you not like to use the service again?'*. You must always remember, however, not to come across as too pushy or combative in your questioning as this can make participants feel that they are under pressure to provide you with a specific answer.

Structured interviews

In a structured interview all the questions are fixed and set beforehand (for example *how many text messages do you send per week?*) and there are a set number of responses that respondents can choose from when they answer the questions (for example, *'please specify how many calls you make per week using your mobile phone: 0–10, 11–20, 21–30, 31–40, 41–50, other amount …'*). However, structured interviews can also contain open questions too (for example, *'are there any other comments that you would like to make about the automated cinema booking service?'*). As this is a very popular form of data collection used in student projects, let's look at how to develop a structured interview form in Technical Tip 3.

Technical Tip 3

Developing a structured interview form

In the study you are about to undertake – looking at metaphors for speech-based mobile phone services – you are interested in finding out some background information from the participants. This will include information such as how many text (or sms) messages they send every day and how many phone calls they make per week. As well as this, you want to find out demographic details of respondents to allow you to look for differences in usage and requirements in relation to age or gender. You could say that you are trying to construct a *'technographic'* structured-interview sheet. The structured interview sheet you could construct may look something like that shown in Figure 3.8.

Participant ID: ....

1. Gender:

male	
female	

2. What age group do you belong to?

18–29	
30–39	
40–49	
50–59	
60–69	
70+	

3. How long have you owned a mobile phone?

less than 6 months	
7 months–1 year	
1 year–1.5 years	
1.5 years–2 years	
more than 2 years	

4. How many text messages (sms messages) do you send per day?

0–10	
11–20	
21–30	
30+	

5. How many mobile phone calls do you make per day?

0–10	
11–20	
21–30	
30+	

6. What type of mobile phone contract do you have?

Pay as you go	
Contract	

Figure 3.8 A structured interview sheet for recording participants' technographic details

7. Which of the following services do you use?

Txt (sms) messages	
WAP services	
Voice mail	
Email	
Picture messaging	
Other (please specify)	

8. Please state how often you use these services per week

Txt (sms) messages	
WAP services	
Voice mail	
Email	
Picture messaging	
Other (please specify)	

Figure 3.8   (*Continued*)

Once you have developed your structured interview sheet, check it over once more (or get a friend or you supervisor to do this) in order to make sure you have the asked the right questions for the technographic data that you are interested in collecting. The next step is to pose the questions to the people who have agreed to take part in your study. One thing to note here is that the reason why you include option lists such as those shown in Figure 3.8, is that if you just asked the question, '*which services do you use on your mobile phone?*', people may not remember all the services that they use.

Once you have collected the data you should put it into a data spreadsheet. You could put it in the same spreadsheet as any other data that you collect from the participants, such as performance measures.

The next step would be to investigate the relationships between technographic information and performance data. For example, whether or not there were differences in the mobile phone behaviour of young people and old people in terms of frequency of use of services such as WAP and voice mail. If this was the case, you might then want to try and explore why these differences occurred.

Diary study

In a diary study, you ask participants to keep a personal record of their thoughts and feelings about interacting with a particular piece of mobile technology; for example, over a certain period of time. This can provide a rich source of textual data for you to analyse. The key thing to remember here is that you have to give participants in your diary study specific instructions of what you want them to describe and write about. Let's look at this in a bit more detail in Technical Tip 4.

Technical Tip 4

Diary study information to participants

The aim of your study is to investigate what teenagers aged 14–16 use their mobiles phones for. In a study such as this, the first thing you would have to do is to provide information for the children's parents explaining the exact nature of your study. This will include how you will collect the data and what you will do with it once you have collected and analysed it.

Once you have obtained permission from their parents you would then approach potential participants (perhaps through their school) and explain the nature of the study to them. If they agree to take part you should ask them to sign an informed consent form (see Chapter 7 for information on constructing informed consent forms).

The next step is to explain to them how you want them to use their diaries to record their data. In order to do this, you could provide them with the instruction sheet shown in Figure 3.9.

You would then specify the duration of the data collection period. One thing to bear in mind is that this approach will generate a large amount of data for you to analyse. As before, make sure that you give yourself sufficient time to collect and analyse the data. For an in-depth discussion on how to analyse this type of data have a look at Silverman (2001) who deals with textual analysis.

Instructions for Making Entries in Your Diary

• Please list the number of text messages (sms's) that you made today and who you sent them to
• Please list the number of mobile phone calls that you made today
• Please list the duration of each call and who you made the call to
• Please list each mobile phone service that you used today and what you think of it
• Please list the locations where you used your phone and what you used it for in these locations
• If you used your phone in a public place, write down how you felt about using it in each of these places

---

Figure 3.9 Instruction sheet

Triangulation

As you can see from above, there are a number of tools and techniques available to you when you want to undertake mobile HCI research. One last thing that's worth mentioning here is that it is often worthwhile considering using multiple research methods when carrying out your research to give you a better understanding of user behaviour. This is known as *triangulation*. In order to do this you have to combine a range of objective and subjective data collection techniques. For example, imagine you are interested in looking at the navigation patterns of a group of users who are using a location-based tourist information guide, accessing it through their mobile phones. In order to get as much information as possible, you may consider using a combination of techniques such as logging how long it takes participants to complete a task, observing them using the service as they go around the city. Afterwards, you could use a Likert-type questionnaire to find out specific information about their attitude towards the usability of the service, afterwards.

SUMMARY

The aim of this chapter was to give you some idea of the generic research tools and techniques that are available to you when it comes to undertaking a mobile HCI research project. In the next chapter we will look at more specific HCI research techniques.

In an interesting and informative review of research methods used in mobile HCI research Kjeldskov and Graham (2003) found that there seemed to be a bias towards research focused on developing systems (e.g. developing interface styles for mobile phone services) and evaluating these prototype designs in a lab setting using traditional evaluation techniques. However, one thing that should become clear as you read this book is the idea that in order to fully understand the utility and effectiveness of mobile systems, there is a need for researchers to broaden their horizons in terms of the research methods they employ. As these systems are mobile, there should be a push towards conducting more research in the context in which these systems will actually be used. This will require us to use some of the techniques discussed in this chapter such as diary studies and field studies. In addition, there is also scope for triangulation here too. For example, after developing an initial interaction technique for a mobile phone service in the lab, it would seem more natural to progress to a field context in order to evaluate this interface. Ultimately, it is up to you to ensure that you choose research methods that are appropriate for the purposes of your study and the type of mobile device or application you want to examine.

Self test

- Independent variable
- Dependent variable
- Matched-pairs design
- Scaler questionnaire
- Field experiment
- Triangulation

Exercises

1. You have just started work as a usability engineer for a mobile phone company. For your first project, you have to design a requirements gathering tool that will provide the designers in your team with information on the features that members of the public would like to have in a new location-based local information service guide.

2. You have to set up a study to investigate the effects of individual differences, such as age, on people's attitude towards a speech-based interface versus a key pad entry interface for a new mobile phone messaging service. What will be your independent and dependent variables in this study?

REFERENCES

Coolican, H. (2000) *Research Methods and Statistics in Psychology.* Hodder and Stoughton

Kjeldskov, J. and Graham C. (2003) A review of mobile HCI research methods. In *Proceedings of the Fifth International Symposium on Mobile HCI*, pp. 317–335

Likert, R. (1932) A technique for the measurement of attitudes. *Archives of Psychology*, No. 140, pp. 1–55

Ling, R. (2002) The social juxtaposition of mobile telephone conversations and public spaces. In *The Social Consequences of Mobile Telephones*, Kim, S.D. (Ed.), Chunchon, Korea

Love, S., Foster, J.C. and Jack, M.A. (1997) Assaying and isolating individual difference in automated telephone services. *Proceedings of the 16th International Symposium on Human Factors in Telecommunications (HFT '97)*, pp. 323–330

Nielson, J. (1993) *Usability Engineering*. Cambridge: MA. Academic Press

Osgood, C.E., Suci, G.J. and Tannenbaum, P.H. *The Measurement of Meaning*. Urbana: University of Illinois Press, 1957

Silverman, D. (2001) *Interpreting Qualitative Data: methods for analysing, talk, text and interaction*. Sage Publications, London

SUGGESTED FURTHER READING

Howitt, D. and Cramer, D. (2000) *An Introduction to Statistics in Psychology: a complete guide for students*. Prentice Hall

Rubin, J. (1994) *Handbook of Usability Testing*. John Wiley and Sons

4

HCI research methods

INTRODUCTION

The aim of this chapter is to introduce to some of the major research methods that can be used in mobile HCI research. This will focus particularly on verbal protocols, heuristics and cognitive walkthroughs. For a comprehensive review of other specific HCI research methods have a look at the further reading section at the end of this chapter for guidance.

VERBAL PROTOCOLS

The idea of using verbal protocols as a form of usability evaluation was originally put forward by Ericsson and Simon (1985). The idea behind this is that it could potentially provide you, the researcher or usability professional, with information on what the user is actually thinking about when they are interacting with a service. Researchers will often use some form of verbal protocol in conjunction with observational data in order to get as much information as possible from the participant in the study.

What kind of information could you get from this form of data collection? Well you may find out how a person is going to tackle a particular task that you have asked them to perform. For example, by adopting this approach, you may discover what menu items are not as clearly worded as they could be, by the user talking about the problems they are having in choosing the correct menu item. In addition, it may let you know that the navigation structure is not as clear-cut as you originally thought it was. You may also get feedback on their subjective feelings at particular points in the interaction, especially if the system does something they didn't expect or they ended up somewhere that they didn't want to be.

This particular kind of verbal protocol technique is known as the '*think aloud*' protocol.

Think aloud protocol

Imagine you have designed a new PDA information service that requires touch screen input (using a stylus pen) and you are interested in finding out users' perceptions of the usability of this service. As part of your data collection exercise, you could adopt the think aloud protocol. The think aloud protocol will be used in this instance to ask people to talk out loud whilst they are completing the task you have given them. The idea is to ask them to tell you what they are thinking about throughout the process.

Although this is a useful form of data collection, it can be a tricky process as some people may find it difficult to talk out loud and complete the task at the same time and other people may just feel embarrassed about the idea of this right from the start. In order to get the most from this process, let's have a look at Technical Tip 1.

Technical Tip 1

Using the think aloud method

1. The key to success in using this method is practice. You must give your participants practice in using the method before data collection begins. One way of doing this is to get your participants to tell you how many doors they have in their house. This will help participants to get into the habit of 'thinking aloud' about a task you have given them. In addition, it will also help them get used to talking out loud in the lab environment.
2. The next step is to give them a practice session using the system they are going to evaluate. If there are any silences at this point you can gently remind them to tell you what they are thinking.
3. Before you start the actual study, ask participants if they know what they have to do and also if it's ok for you to audio record their thoughts, feelings, etc. in the course of the trial.

4. Throughout the trial, make sure you get participants to talk but don't be too overbearing. Just give them gentle reminders.
5. Once the trial is over, you will need to transcribe the audio recording to analyse the data you have collected.

Another form of verbal protocol data collection that you may find useful is called the *post-event protocols*. In this situation you bring participants back into your lab after they have completed a study or trial and ask them to provide information on the tasks they were asked to carry out as part of the study. If you made a video recording of their session, the participants can do this by going through it with you, while providing you with a running commentary of the reasons for their actions when they were carrying out the tasks that you asked them to complete. They can also provide you with information on their subjective feelings as they went through this process. If you used an audio recording, then you can use this method too – in this instance, you would go through the same process that I have just outlined above. In addition, if you have looked at the participants' sessions and there are specific aspects you want to focus on (e.g. a menu link that was causing most participants problems) then you could only play these parts and ask for feedback. Monk *et al.* (1993) suggest that this is a very useful method as it can stimulate a participant to inform you of any particular problems that they had with the system (and they didn't verbalise during the think aloud procedure) and it could also highlight particular parts of the interface that they thought were very usable.

HEURISTICS

Heuristic evaluation was developed by Molich and Nielson (1990) to assess key areas of usability for a system or prototype. A heuristic is a principle that is used in making a decision. The idea behind heuristic evaluation is that several people (known as *evaluators*) independently carry out a usability evaluation of a system or prototype to identify any potential problems with the design, using a known list of design heuristics as an aid. These evaluators should not only identify and list the usability problems of the system or prototype but they should also indicate the *severity* of the problem too. One thing to notice about heuristics is that they are related to design principles and guidelines (which is discussed in Chapter 5), as it makes sense to evaluate a system on these principles. In addition, heuristic evaluation is normally conducted at an early stage of evaluation, before users are involved in the evaluation process.

According to Nielson and Landauer (1993), you only need five heuristic evaluators to take part in this exercise as they will normally identify about 75 per cent of the usability problems that your prototype or system has. This makes it very cost-effective process. For example, most evaluations can be carried out in a couple of hours and each evaluator only needs a problem sheet to complete and a copy of the system or prototype that they have to evaluate.

So what are these heuristics principles that we should use to evaluate our system or prototype? According to Preece *et al.* (1994, p. 676), they are as follows:

- use simple dialogue that users can understand
- do not overload users' working memory
- consistency
- provide feedback to the user
- provide good error messages
- prevent errors
- provide short cuts
- provide clearly marked exits.

One question that is of interest to us here is: do these heuristics cover the needs for an analysis of mobile technologies? According to Barber (2001) two other heuristics could be added to this list if you want to accommodate mobile technologies needs. These are: *appropriate modes of use and structure of information*. One can see the importance of these for mobile technologies. For example, if you are in a noisy public place such as a café, and you are trying to access your voice mail on your mobile phone it makes sense to be able to move from speech-input to keypad entry to find out why your friend is late. In relation to the structure of information it is also important considering the limitations of our working memory (remember we spoke about this in Chapter 2) that people do not have to listen to long menu lists; for example, when they are using mobile phone services such as a train timetable and booking service.

There are, however, some limitations that have been identified with heuristic evaluation. According to Bailey (2001), for every correct usability problem identified by heuristic evaluation, there were on average almost one and a half false alarms recorded. Andre (2001) also pointed out that the expertise of the evaluators is also of importance in helping to obtain reliable and accurate information.

Therefore, if you are going to use this method effectively, it is important that your evaluators are experienced mobile HCI practitioners or researchers. In addition, they all have to agree on the definition of each heuristic that you have on your problem definition sheet.

To give you a better idea of what is meant by a problem sheet I've included one in Technical Tip 2.

Technical Tip 2

Heuristic evaluation sheet

Imagine that for your research project you have designed a PDA application that allows you to access your university's student handbook and services such as the library (renewing books, etc.) and the time and location for your lectures. Your problem sheet may look something like Figure 4.1.

One thing that is worth noting is that this example is designed to provide a high level of heuristic analysis of the system as a whole. When it comes

Heuristic	Problem Severity		
Visual feedback from system	Low	Medium	High
User control and freedom	Low	Medium	High
Consistency	Low	Medium	High
Error messages	Low	Medium	High
Exit from system clearly marked	Low	Medium	High
Provision of shortcuts	Low	Medium	High
Structure of information	Low	Medium	High
Icons	Low	Medium	High
Help facility	Low	Medium	High
Font size	Low	Medium	High
Dialogue style	Low	Medium	High
Other (specify)	Low	Medium	High
Additional Comments			

Figure 4.1   Sample of a Heuristic Evaluation Sheet

to conducting your own heuristic analysis you may want a more detailed level of analysis on specific pages or specific screens.

Once you have completed this form the idea is that you aggregate your results with the other evaluators to produce an overall heuristic evaluation which should highlight the system's key weaknesses.

COGNITIVE WALKTHROUGH

Like heuristic evaluation, the cognitive walkthrough is a form of system or prototype usability evaluation carried out by experts. This approach was developed by Polson *et al.* (1992) who were interested in the cognitive activities of the user when they are carrying out a *specific task.* The focus of the cognitive walkthrough is on how easy the users will find it to learn, and how to use the system in an effective, efficient and satisfying way. It assesses each step a user is required to perform by the system in order to complete a task. Therefore, the role of the evaluator is to walkthrough each step in turn and assess whether or not it meets those users' needs.

Technical Tip 3 will explain what you need to do in order to conduct a cognitive walkthrough.

Technical Tip 3

Conducting a cognitive walkthrough

In order to conduct a cognitive walkthrough you need to ensure the following:

1. You have to give the evaluators a copy of the system or prototype or provide them with a detailed description of this. In addition, you should provide the evaluators with a task that is representative of the actual tasks that people will carry out when using the fully implemented version of the system.
2. In relation to this, you should provide the evaluators with a list of instructions on what they should do in order to complete each part of the task.
3. You should also provide the evaluators with information on the people who you envisage will use this system or service once it is fully functional. This could include information such as their age and experience of using this kind of service or system.

The best way to carry out these steps would be to provide evaluators with an information sheet such as this:

Task scenario

The user has to use the mobile phone provided to find out if the automated music catalogue has the cd '*By the Way*', by the Red Hot Chilli Peppers and which they would like to purchase, is in stock. The automated music catalogue service requires speech input from the user.

User characteristics
It is envisaged that this service will be used by anyone over the age of 18 years of age who has a mobile phone and has experience of using automated services via their mobile phones.

Intended priming instructions for participants
* The automated music catalogue service allows you to order cds from our wide range of artists, albums and music categories.
* To help you make your selection, the service lets you listen to short extracts of the music of your choice.
* At each point, the service will offer you choices. Listen carefully and respond by saying the name of the item you want to select. If you make a mistake or do not say anything the service will ask you to try again. If you know which item you want to select, you can say the name of the item before the voice finishes.
* At any time you can say the word 'options' to obtain more information from the service. This includes information on how to hear menu options again and how to leave the automated music catalogue service.

Task completion actions
1. The participant has to listen to the six categories of music that are available from this service (Blues, Jazz, Classical, Rock & Pop, R&B, Soul)
2. Next, the participant chooses a category of music (in this case, Rock & Pop)
3. The participant then has to listen to the list of artists available in this category and choose the ones they have been asked to find (in this instance, the Red Hot Chilli Peppers)
4. The participant then chooses a cd by the artists from a list of four (in this instance, *By the Way*)
5. They then listen to a short excerpt from one of the tracks on this cd (in this instance, *Cabron*)
6. The participant then adds the cd to their shopping trolley

<table>
<tr><td colspan="5">Evaluators Observations</td></tr>
</table>

Name ....

Date ....

Action	Finding	Generating	Navigation	Other
1				
2				
3				
4				
5				
6				
7				
8				
9				

Figure 4.2   Sample of an Observation Form

7. The participant then pays for the cd and completes their delivery information and payment details
8. The participant exits the service.

After completing each action in the above sequence please assess it, using the following three categories.

1. ***Finding***
    Finding information relates to the process whereby participants find the correct category of music, the correct artist within that category of music and the correct album by the artist they are interested in.
2. ***Generating***
    Generating can be defined as the process which allows participants to generate the correct action to allow them to access the information they were looking for.

3. *Navigation*

Navigation refers to the process which allows participants to move around the database structure of the automated music catalogue service. For example, after choosing to purchase a cd by a particular artist in a specific music category, participants should be able to navigate their way to another category of music that they can browse in.

It is important that the evaluator includes both the good things as well as the problems that they would envisage participants having when they were trying to complete this given task. A sample observation form is shown in Figure 4.2.

Once all the evaluators have completed their observation sheets, the data should be aggregated to provide the researcher with an overall picture of what the evaluators imagine the main problems users will have when trying to complete the tasks set, given the current design of the automated music catalogue service. In addition, it will also highlight what, if any, aspects of the service design work well.

The cognitive walkthrough approach belongs to a range of evaluation techniques that come under the generic name of *task analysis*. Essentially, task analysis is concerned with breaking down each task into a series of detailed actions and highlighting any problems in the action sequence that the evaluator envisages a user would have trying to complete a specific task. For example, another well-known type of task analysis is *hierarchical task analysis*.

Any usability and functional problems that are identified using task analysis techniques should be accommodated for in the next phase of the prototype or product development cycle. Chapter 5 looks at prototyping techniques for mobile devices. However, in the Further Reading section at the end of this chapter you will be directed to several texts which provide an in-depth coverage of other HCI research techniques.

SUMMARY

The aim of this chapter has been to provide you with an introduction to some of the specific HCI research evaluation techniques you could use as part of your own research studies. To begin with we looked at verbal protocols and, in particular, the think aloud protocol. This technique can be particularly useful if you have mobile devices you want to evaluate in lab settings. Next we moved on to talk about heuristic evaluation. Unlike verbal protocol data collection, this technique relies on getting data from a small group of experts. However, a key component in the successful use of this technique is getting people who are sufficiently experienced to carry out the evaluation as well as having a clear idea of the heuristics your evaluators are going to use to assess the interface design.

Finally, I described in detail how to conduct a form of task analysis known as the cognitive walkthrough. Like the heuristic evaluation method, this approach is carried out by expert evaluators working to a given set of guidelines. However, unlike heuristic analysis, a cognitive walkthrough analysis provides a more detailed level of analysis by breaking each task down into a series of action sequences that the user has to complete in order to achieve their overall goal.

As with the general research methods I discussed in the previous chapter, when it comes to using techniques such as the ones I have described in this chapter, it is important you choose them on the basis of what your project aims and objectives are. In addition, you should consider whether or not you will have the resources to use them (e.g. can you get five experts to help you with your evaluation?)

Self test

- Think aloud protocol
- Heuristic evaluation
- Cognitive walkthrough
- Post-event protocols

Exercises

1. You want to evaluate an interface which you have developed a PDA application for, and which will be used by a mobile health worker (e.g. district nurse) to enter details of the treatments they administer to their patients when doing their rounds. Adopting a cognitive walkthrough evaluation approach, develop an information sheet for your expert evaluators to use for this assessment.

2. As part of your data collection exercise to evaluate a new PDA application that will access sports information, describe and document in detail how you will use the think aloud protocol as a method of data collection.

REFERENCES

Andre, T.S. (2001) The user action framework: a reliable foundation for usability engineering support tools. *International Journal of Human–Computer Studies*, Vol. 54, pp. 107–136. London: Academic Press

Bailey, R.W. (2001) Heuristic evaluation vs user testing. UI design update newsletter – January 2001. http://www.humanfactors.com/library/jan001.htm

Barber, C. (2001) *An Interactive Heuristic Evaluation Toolkit*. Master's Project, University of Sussex, UK. http://www.id-book.com/catherb/index.htm

Ericsson, K.A. and Simon, H.A. (1985) *Protocol Analysis: verbal reports as data*. Cambridge MA: MIT Press

Molich, R. and Nielson, J. (1990) Improving a human–computer dialogue. *Communications of the ACM*, **33**(3), 338–348

Monk, A., Wright, P., Haber, J. and Davenport, L. (1993) *Improving your Human–Computer Interface: a practical technique*. New York: Prentice Hall

Nielson, J. and Landauer, T.K. (1993) A mathematical model of finding of usability problems. *Proceedings of INTERACT 1993*, pp. 206–213. New York: Academic Press

Nielson, J. (1994) Heuristic Evaluation. In *Usability Inspection Methods*. John Wiley, New York

Polson, P.G., Lewis, C., Rieman, J. and Wharton, C. (1992) Cognitive walk-throughs: a method for theory-based evaluation of users interfaces. *International Journal of Man–Machine Studies*, **36**, 741–773

Preece, J., Rogers, Y., Benyon, D., Holland, S. and Carey, T. (1994) *Human–Computer Interaction*. Addison-Wesley

FURTHER READING

Diaper, D. (1989) *Task Analysis for Human–computer Interaction*. Chichester: Ellis Horwood

Dix, A., Finlay, J., Abowd, G. and Beale, R. (2004), *Human–Computer Interaction*, 3rd Edition. Chapter 7. Prentice Hall

Preece, J., Rogers, Y., Sharp, H., Benyon, D., Holland, S. and Carey, T. (1994) *Human–Computer Interaction*, Chapter 20. Addison-Wesley

Wharton, C., Rieman, J., Lewis, C. and Polson, P. (1994) The cognitive walk-through: a practitioner's guide. In *Usability Inspection Methods*. John Wiley, New York

5

Design issues for mobile systems

INTRODUCTION

This chapter discusses design issues that you should be aware of when developing mobile systems and applications. It starts off by describing an HCD approach to mobile system and application development. After this, the discussion moves on to describing a set of principles that you should take into consideration if you are going to design a mobile service or system. The chapter then focuses on several requirements gathering techniques that can be used as part of a human-centred design approach to mobile applications and systems development. After this, I will describe various interaction styles that are available to mobile application and product developers. Finally, the chapter includes a discussion of the prototyping techniques that you can use when designing these systems. The chapter concludes with a summary.

HUMAN-CENTRED DESIGN

Usability is an essential factor in the design of all successful products. What is usability? Usability refers to whether an application is easy to learn, easy to use, and enjoyable to use for the intended users. The International

Standards Organisation (ISO) published a standard on usability (Ergonomic requirements for office work with visual display terminals (VDTs) – Part II: Guidance on Usability, ISO 9241–11, 1998) which states that usability requirements should be based on providing an effective, efficient and satisfying system for users to interact with. Effectiveness relates to how good the system is at what it is supposed to do (e.g. does the mobile phone service really provide you with all the information you need in relation to booking a cinema ticket?) efficiency relates to whether or not the system supports users in relation to carrying out their tasks (e.g. can you use the menu structure to find out information on forthcoming attractions at the cinema?), and satisfaction relates to people's perception of the system and how easy it is to use.

According to researchers such as Maguire (2001a), the way to achieve a usable system is to adopt an HCD approach to system development. The key concepts behind a human-centred design methodology are described in the ISO Standard 13407 (Human-Centred Design Processes for Inter-active Systems, 1999) on human-centred design. This standard states that there are four key stages in planning a human-centred design process:

1. understand and specify the context of use
2. specify user and organisational requirements
3. produce designs and prototypes
4. undertake user based assessment.

These methods and activities are seen as being part of an iterative design process as Figure 5.1 shows.

In order to understand this ISO standard more clearly, let's have a look at each of the stages in a bit more detail.

Understand and specify the context of use

In the HCD process context of use relates to the physical, social, technical and organisational conditions in which the systems will be used (Maguire, 2001b). The outcome of a context of use analysis should provide the design team with background information that can feed into the design and evaluation stages of your project. For example, imagine you are part of a team that are designing a tourist information guide to be used via a mobile phone; in what kind of contexts and locations do you think an application like this would be used? To begin with, it will be used by people in busy public places such as walking along the street, sitting on

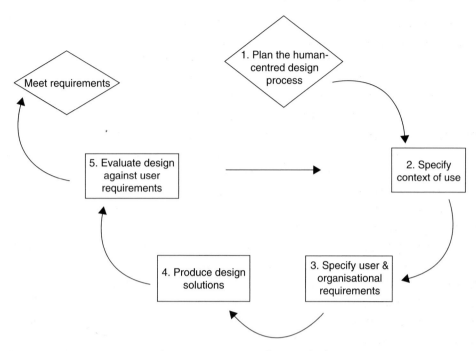

Figure 5.1   Human-Centred Design Activities (ISO 13407)

a crowded train or bus, etc. In addition, people will probably want to use the application indoors, such as in a café, art gallery or a museum. Therefore, the dynamic environments that people will find themselves in when using this type of application is something that needs to be remembered when making design decisions such as: what is the best way for the individual to interact with the service? For example, should the application allow both speech and keypad, as speech may be a more appropriate way to interact with the service in some locations and contexts rather than others (e.g. using the guide to go round an art gallery and provide descriptions of selected paintings)?

Specify user and organisational requirements

User and organisational requirements capture factors such as the characteristics of the intended user group and their needs in relation to the system being developed. The result of this requirements-analysis should be a clear description of the tasks that the system needs to support; including a step-by-step guide of how users will interact with the system. In addition, the results of the requirements-gathering exercise should include a description of the functionality required to support these tasks. This stage should also provide the designer with a clear idea of the potential scenarios in which the application will be used.

How do you go about obtaining these requirements? Well you could start off by conducting a series of interviews (using methods discussed in Chapter 3) with potential users of the system in order to establish their needs. You could also think about using one of the requirements-gathering techniques that are discussed later in this chapter (e.g. card sorting or brainstorming).

In addition, if you are designing a mobile system that will be used in an organisational context, you will need to discover the tasks and activities that people undertake as part of their job in order to ensure that the design meets these requirements. In this context, the requirements-gathering could take the form of interviews with various members of staff and it may also involve observing or 'shadowing' people as they go about their work over a period of several days. This will provide information (and challenges) such as how do you co-ordinate the activities of a team of people if they are mobile and on the road (e.g. television service engineers), and how will the mobile system be able to provide the technical back-up that the workers may require to carry out their jobs effectively (e.g. getting remote access to databases that are located back the firm's headquarters)?.

Produce design solutions

Not surprisingly, there are a number of different designs that can meet a system's specification. However, it is the job of the designer to ensure that the system matches the requirements of the user (or organisation). One way to test design ideas is to develop prototypes and get feedback from users. User feedback can then be used to create a better prototype iteratively. It should also be noted that it is cheaper to discover flaws in a prototype than in a finished product. At a broad level, there are two types of prototyping: paper-based and computer-based (Preece *et al.*, 2002).

Paper-based prototyping is classed as *low fidelity* and includes techniques such as card sorting and sketching which is discussed later in this chapter. These techniques have the advantage of being quick and inexpensive and can be used to provide valuable feedback on the usability of the product or application at an early stage of the design process. In addition, depending on the time and budget constraints of your research project, these types of approaches may be the only option available to you.

On the other hand, computer-based prototyping is classed as high fidelity and provides a system with limited functionality which users can interact with. This allows you to assess its usability. For example, mobile phone emulators which allow you to develop your own prototypes are available on the Internet. Emulators for mobile phones are discussed later in this chapter.

Therefore, if you are adopting an HCD approach to product development, you should include both low fidelity and high fidelity prototyping as part of the design process. You would normally start with low fidelity prototypes and move on to high fidelity prototypes when your criteria are extremely well developed. However, if you are carrying out a mobile HCI research project as part of your studies as a student, your budget and time constraints may limit you to only undertaking low fidelity prototyping.

Evaluation

According to Preece *et al.* (1994) there are four main reasons why people should undertake usability evaluations:

1. to understand how users use technology in the real world
2. to compare different prototype designs
3. to assess whether or not the product or application meets usability requirements
4. to ensure that the product or application conforms to industry standards.

It would be a good idea, especially if you are following an HCD approach, that you start evaluating the design of the product as early as possible in the design process (known as formative evaluation). This ensures that users' needs and abilities are always in the forefront of the design team's thinking. However, it is also important to carry out a final evaluation of the product or application after development has finished to ensure that people can use it successfully (this is known as summative evaluation).

A good evaluation should have a clearly defined set of goals. For example, if you have designed a tourist information guide for a mobile phone, you will have specific questions that you will want to address in the evaluation stage in relation to the application's usability (e.g. can people use it in different locations, how easy is it to get access to the information required). There are four main approaches to the evaluation of systems and applications according to Preece *et al.* (2002) and these can be summarized as follows:

1. '***Quick and dirty approach***': this is a quick and informal approach to getting feedback on initial design ideas. In this evaluation approach, the designer will talk to users about how they plan to design the product and application in order to ensure that they meet with users' needs and expectations.

2. ***Usability testing***: this involves collecting information on users' performance while they are carrying out specific tasks and assessing their attitude towards using a particular product service. The types of measures that can be used in usability testing are discussed in Chapters 3 and 4 of this book and include performance measures such as time taken to complete a task. In addition, in terms of assessing users' attitude towards the application, questionnaires and interviews are commonly used. Most usability testing tasks take place under controlled conditions in a usability lab.

3. ***Field studies***: field studies take place in natural surroundings where the application is designed to be used, with the aim of understanding how the system impacts the user in their everyday context of use. One can see the importance of this evaluation approach in relation to mobile applications and systems. There are various techniques that can be used to gather evaluation information using a field study approach, such as observations and ethnography. These two techniques, as well as others, are discussed in Chapters 3 and 6.

4. ***Predictive evaluation***: in this evaluation approach, experts use their knowledge of users to predict what kinds of problems they may have with a given system or application. Techniques that they may employ here are *task analysis* and *heuristic evaluation*. If you are unsure of these approaches have a look at Chapter 4 to refresh your memory.

PRINCIPLES OF INTERFACE DESIGN FOR MOBILE SYSTEMS

This section focuses on principles of design for mobile applications and systems. Hopefully it will give you an understanding of the various factors that need to be taken into consideration as part of a HCD approach to mobile product development.

Context of use

If you are designing any kind of interactive system (even a prototype for part of your research project), you should be aware of the context in which the service or application will be used. When it comes to designing a mobile service or application you should remember that people will be using these devices in dynamic environments, such as in a crowded café, on the train or at a work location (e.g. an architect on site). In addition, people may experience network connection problems as they move from location to location, thus potentially impacting on the use of their mobile application. Distractions can include walking down the street while trying to use the device, which could cause interaction problems (Brewster, 2002) and/or auditory distractions (e.g. being close to a busy road). The actual presence of someone close to the user may actually put them off or make them feel that they cannot or should not use their device because of the social context. In addition, how will users feel about always being able to be contacted by their boss and their movements being tracked?

Having established the importance of designers being aware of the implications of context of use, let us look at other design principles that you should consider when designing mobile applications and devices.

Consistency and learnability

The mobile interface should meet users' expectations. What does this mean? It means that the interface should be similar to a user's previous experience with similar systems and services. For example, some PDA devices use Microsoft Windows PocketPC which is basically a scaled down version of Microsoft Windows. Therefore, in theory, this should cut down on the amount of time and effort people will have to spend on learning how to manage their files and applications on their PDA device.

Although it can be tempting to design a totally new interface, you must ask yourself whether it will add to or detract from the ease of use of the system. The key thing to remember here is that users do not want to spend a lot of time learning new techniques to help them access information via their PDA unless these techniques are easy to learn and save them time in comparison to the 'old' techniques that they had previously used. For example, some PDA applications allow users to use handwriting technology but this appears to take time to learn and users have to keep practicing in order to use it effectively.

Flexibility

Flexibility is concerned with the way the user and the mobile service or application exchange information interact. You should be aware that different users have different needs and expectations when it comes to using your mobile application or device. Therefore, the design of the system should try and accommodate these differing needs, within reason of course.

For example, imagine you are working as part of a design team for a mobile phone service provider developing an integrated voice messaging service that will include email, sms (text messaging), voice mail and fax facilities. The service will use speech input and speech output. A business user can be reasonably expected to use all of these services on a regular basis. Therefore, they should be able to 'fast track' through or take the initiative in any system dialogues to get to the information or service that they require as quickly and efficiently as possible. On the other hand, a user who only occasionally uses the voice mail part of this service can reasonably be expected to let the system take the initiative and lead them to where they want to go.

Another dimension to flexibility is the exchange of information between different platforms such as downloading an application or information from the internet from your desktop PC on to your PDA. Although it is good idea to be able to exchange information across platforms, the key thing to remember here are the limitations of the PDA device (e.g. small screen size, memory size, limited input style) and design accordingly. In addition, ensure you conform to any industry standards.

System feedback and support

The system interface should provide the user with enough information to enable them to complete tasks in an effective and efficient way. This should include appropriate feedback from the system so the user knows what is happening; such as answering the user's concerns about 'Where am I?', 'What can I do next?', 'How do I get there?'. In relation to this, one of the common problems associated with interacting with mobile phone services is getting lost in a hierarchy of menus and sub-menus that must be navigated in order to reach the information or service they are looking for. Brewster (1997) argues that navigation information for phone-based interfaces should be kept to a minimum because it can get 'in the way' of the information or services that users are trying to access and this could result in feelings of increased frustration. The same can be said to be true for mobile applications.

It is also very important that the system is supportive of the mobile user if they lose their wireless connection when interacting with the service. For example, consider the case of the mobile health worker (e.g. district nurse) making a home visit. The PDA application allows the nurse to enter the patient's personal details, diagnosis and treatments. This information is automatically entered into a database back at the health centre. What if, as the nurse is entering the diagnosis for a patient, temporary wireless connection is lost? If you have designed a truly supportive system, when the wireless connection returns, and the service should provide feedback to the nurse that it is ok to continue to enter their information without the need to re-enter any information.

MOBILE INTERACTION STYLES

Having discussed the principles of design for mobile systems, this section moves on to discuss various interaction styles that are available for users of mobile products, services and applications. When users are interacting with mobile applications and devices there are a limited number of styles available to them. Let's have a look at these interaction styles in a bit more detail.

Text entry

The input styles available to the user are as follows, depending on the device and application: keyboard entry (if the device supports this), touch screen (using a stylus) handwriting technology or using the numbered keys on the keypad (i.e. typical mobile phone format). A key point to remember here is that the context of use may make it difficult for the user to make certain forms of text entry. For example, if the user is on a train and they pick up their PDA to write up some notes from a meeting they have just attended, they may have to wait until there is enough space at the table before they can get their detachable keyboard out and connect it. Alternatively, if the user has access to handwriting technology to input the notes of their meeting they will have to make sure that they have been practicing this technique frequently or it could be a long process.

In addition to this, there are content issues to consider. For example, if someone on a train wishes to access an application on their PDA which requires them to make a number of selections from menu options, it may be more practical for them to use some type of touch screen (with a stylus) selection rather than having to type on a keyboard.

The key thing to remember here is the application's context of use and try to accommodate for the needs of the users in these myriad of situations by allowing them to adapt to an input style that is most suited to their current needs.

Speech input

Another form of interaction is based on speech input, which relies on the speech recognition technology of the mobile phone application the user is currently using.

One of the clearest descriptions of the challenges of designing effective speech recognition systems has been provided by Bristow (1986) who used a toothpaste analogy. Bristow suggested that speech output was similar to squeezing the tube to get the toothpaste out, whereas speech input was a bit like trying to put the toothpaste back in again. Speech recognition systems generally fall into two categories: *speaker-dependent* and *speaker-independent*.

√ *Speaker-dependent*

Speaker-dependent systems require the user to speak a sample of words they will use when interacting with the service through a process known as *enrolment*. This may require the user to repeat the words several times in order to provide the system with a template for their voice. Perhaps you may have used one of these systems in the form of a word processing package that you train to recognise your voice?

Speaker-independent

Speaker-independent systems on the other hand, do not use a template from a single user. The vocabulary accepted by this type of system has been pre-defined from a large number of speech samples taken from a cross-section of the target population.

As you may expect, speaker-dependent systems have a greater recognition accuracy than speaker-independent systems. Noyes (2001) highlights the fact that current speaker-independent recognition systems have problems handling large vocabularies and multiple word input. This finding is supported by the fact that many speech-based automated phone services use a numbered menu style. This constrains the options that the user can use (e.g. 'for cinema listings, say 1, for ticket prices, say 2') resulting in high recognition rates but longer interaction times, which will have an impact on the user's mobile phone bill.

Another important area to consider here, are the menu issues in relation to automated mobile phone services. Let's consider these in a bit more detail.

Menu issues for automated mobile phone services

Automated mobile phone services usually have a structured menu hierarchy but do not always provide the user with navigational tips. For example, people can call an automated mobile phone service that has a long list of menu choices, but which overloads the user's short-term memory (if you are not sure about this term, refer back to Chapter 2 on individual indifferences) and as a result they become lost, confused and irritated with the system.

Why is this a problem? Because of the difference between speech interfaces and graphical user interfaces. A graphical user interface (GUI) can display information via graphics, text, icons, menus, video and audio. These different modes can be used as short-term memory aids and navigational cues; for example, the user can scan menu lists until they find the option they require. However, with a speech-based interface, there are no short-term memory aids and information can only be presented in a serial fashion.

Therefore speech systems have a dual function: providing information and navigation cues. This, according to Brewster (1997) is the main cause of navigational problems associated with speech-based phone services.

So how can these short-term memory overload problems be addressed? Three approaches that could help reduce this burden on the user are: conversational dialogues, earcons and metaphors. Let's have a look at each of these in turn.

Conversational interfaces

The best way to define a conversational style dialogue is to give you a description of one of the earliest examples of this kind of interface style. Schmandt (1987) described an automated telephone service called the *Phone Slave* which was an answering machine service that allowed users to retrieve stored messages. The system worked on the basis of asking the caller a series of questions like 'who's calling please?' and 'what's this in reference to?'. The Phone Slave has no understanding of the content of the messages left by any of the callers. The users' responses were stored digitally by the service and could be accessed in sequential order by the system's owner. For example, the owner could ask the service 'who left messages?' and the system would respond by playing back all the responses to its own query 'who's calling please?'.

Schmandt found that the interface was very effective in eliciting appropriate voice message components from callers, attributing the success of the conversational style to the apparent high quality of the spoken prompts provided by the system. To take a message requires co-operative behaviour and there is no reason to think that callers will not follow conventional rules. By asking a series of questions, as opposed to a message such as 'leave your message after the beep', the system makes it easier for the user to leave a more complete message as a series of components. In doing so, the system maintains its ability to control the conversation and protects the system's limited 'intelligence' from being exposed.

Other examples of this type of approach can be seen with the Philips TABA train timetable information service (Souvignier *et al.*, 2000) and the SpeechWorks air travel reservation system (Barnard *et al.*, 1999). Both these systems rely on system initiated dialogue to keep the speech recognition accuracy levels high.

However, there are still some problems to be overcome for natural language conversational interfaces, such as increasing the number of words that can successfully be recognised as a part of the service's vocabulary, and effective recovery methods when misrecognition occurs. It's important that the service gets the user back on track and that the user has confidence in the system's ability to understand what they are saying.

Earcons

Blattner *et al.* (1989) define earcons as being abstract musical tones that can be combined to produce sound messages to represent parts of an interface. They have been found to be effective in communicating information (Brewster *et al.*, 1993) and navigational cues in non-visual interfaces (Brewster *et al.*, 1996).

In relation to mobile phone service design in a study looking at the limited feedback given on the screens of mobile phone interfaces, Leplatre and Brewster (2000) found that menus augmented with earcons produced better results in user-performance than those found for the visual-only version of the interface.

This would seem to suggest that earcons can play a significant role in improving navigation with speech-based mobile phone services. However, the impact of earcons has been limited. Reasons for this could be due to background noise when using a mobile phone in a public place such as a train, or it could be related to the problems with network connections in a mobile environment which can lead to degradation in the sound quality.

Metaphors

The idea of using a metaphor for designing interfaces can be traced back to the design of the Xerox Star graphical user interface (Smith *et al.*, 1982). This was the birth of the desktop metaphor with which we are now so familiar. An interface metaphor works by applying prior knowledge from a familiar domain to a new domain. In the case of the desktop metaphor the physical components of the office, such as files, folders and wastepaper baskets, were used as the cognitive and visual framework for the organisation and representation of information on the computer. The emphasis was on users thinking about interface objects in physical terms. Interface metaphors were (and still are) regarded by companies such as Apple as the way to reduce people's perception of the complexity of the system they are using.

Another example of applying prior knowledge from familiar domains to a computer-based environment can be seen in the shopping trolleys or shopping baskets found in online shopping environments. Once people have all the items they want in their shopping basket, they can proceed to the check-out where they pay for their goods. This metaphor is widely understood and accepted by online shoppers.

However, according to Marcus (2002) the desktop metaphor is no longer appropriate for new technologies and interaction paradigms. He backs this up by pointing to the fact that new paradigms such as Computer

Supported Collaborative work (CSCW) and virtual reality have extended the task environment from the user's desk to organisations working together and users interacting at different locations. So what are the implications for mobile technologies and applications?

The first thing to notice is that mobile systems are often used in environments that are very different from the desktop environment (for example, a mobile health worker updating information into their internet-enabled PDA device while making a home visit). Apart from the environment itself, the actual size of the device with its reduced screen size, has led to the development of new mobile metaphors. For example, laptop computers can be based on a book metaphor (e.g. Apple Power-Book) and PDAs such as the PalmPilot, have been designed with a pen and paper metaphor in mind.

There have also been metaphors developed for PDAs that rely on gestural and audio cues. For example, Pirhonen and Brewster (2002) developed a method of controlling a digital music player accessed via a PDA, by using gestural and audio cues. The aim behind this was to provide the user with a non-visual means of interacting with the system, thus allowing them to pay full attention to their current physical environment. Moving their hand across the screen from left to right would allow the user to start a track, and moving it in the opposite direction would activate the previous track.

Another approach to developing metaphors for mobile applications has been discussed by Howell *et al.* (2005). This study compared the usability of a metaphor-based version of a speech-activated mobile city guide service (known as the office filing system service) and a standard speech-based service. The affects of individual differences (such as age, gender and cognitive skills) on attitude towards and performance with the mobile services were also explored. A Wizard of Oz methodology was used to provide the service functionality for both versions of the mobile city guide service. All participants completed tasks over a six week period in both public and private locations.

The results obtained from this study suggest that the office filing service may be better able to accommodate users' individual differences than the standard service; that context of use affects the patterns with which individual differences affect performance and attitude with the standard service; and that, for the standard service, users' individual differences are more likely to affect their attitudes than their performance. The results support the use of interface metaphor to improve the usability of speech-based automated phone services for a larger number of potential users. Therefore, one advantage that appears to emerge from the research literature is that the application of metaphors in interface design helps users to improve performance and learn how to use the system in a more effective, efficient and satisfying way.

USER-CENTRED REQUIREMENT GATHERING TECHNIQUES

This section of the chapter describes several requirements gathering techniques that you may find useful when undertaking a human-centred design approach to mobile application and product development. It should be noted that taking the user into consideration should not be seen as optional; after all, if they can't use it or don't like your service why would they want it?

Card Sorting

If you want to adhere to the human-centred design process that we spoke about at the beginning of this chapter, you need to think about ways in which you can allow participants to represent their 'mental model' of the mobile service or application (i.e. what they think the service structure looks like). One technique that allows you to do this is card sorting. This technique does not impose the structure of the service on to participants or users (in the form of a structured diagram). Instead they are asked to create their own structure. Card sorting is quick, easy and cheap to carry out.

The results of card sorting are often used to produce the first simple prototype in the iterative design cycle. Essentially, it is an elicitation technique for grouping information into categories from an unsorted list of statements or ideas (McDonald and Schvaneveldt, 1988). Thus, card sorting allows the designer to investigate how participants group items in order to develop a service structure that reflects their needs. This should increase the probability of users being able to find the information they are looking for (in theory anyway). Card sorting offers, according to Rosenfeld and Morville (1998), the designer an insight into how real users organise information and structure information spaces in their own head. In addition, it also provides designers with information on what items users have difficulty categorising. So how would one go about undertaking a card sorting exercise? Let's look at this in Technical Tip 1.

Technical Tip 1

Card sorting

1. The scenario is that you are interested in designing a new mobile phone-based tourist information guide.
2. Gather your participants together in a room and introduce the scenario (e.g. designing a new mobile phone-based tourist information guide).
3. Arrange the participants into small groups (e.g. about three or four per group).
4. Present each group with a set of cards. Each card should have written on it the name of a menu item that could be included in the new service. An example of the items you could include on the cards are as follows:
   - Welcome message
   - Entertainment
   - Pubs
   - Clubs
   - Restaurants
   - Cinemas
   - Leisure centres.
5. You may also include several blank cards to provide participants with the opportunity to add menu items of their own.
6. Participants should then be told that they have to arrange the cards into a potential structure for the new mobile phone service. It is important at this stage to inform participants that there is no right way or wrong way to go about this task. They should be told that all they have to do is to arrange the cards into a structure that makes sense to their group.
7. It may be a good idea to impose some kind of time limit on this exercise, such as 30 minutes. This may vary, of course, depending on the size of the service you are designing (i.e. the larger the service, the more cards that will need sorting into categories).
8. After the card sorting exercise has been completed, the next step is to get participants to explain how they would access the different sources of information contained in the tourist information guide, using their service design. This can be done by getting one member of each group to go through a representative task (e.g. how do I find out where the cinemas are?).
9. The last item is important to include as part of your card sorting exercise, as it addresses two of the major disadvantages associated with this approach: participants not really considering what the content is, or how they would actually go about using their design to accomplish a task.

Another technique which can be used to explore participants' ideas of the spatial structure of the service is *sketching*.

Sketching

The idea behind sketching (not surprisingly) is to get participants to sketch what they imagine the structure of the service to be like, rather than sorting cards. Once again, you could get participants to explain to you the reasons why they designed the system in a specific way. You may also wish to ask them to complete a task using their own service design. One potential drawback with this approach is if your participants may have poor drawing skills. You must ask them to clarify any aspects of their sketch of the system that appears unclear to you.

Brainstorming

Like card sorting and sketching, brainstorming can be useful in the early stages of the design process, especially when the goal is to develop a new system. This technique has been around for a long time and is regarded as being very useful in facilitating the development of creative design ideas (e.g. Osborn, 1963). Essentially, this approach requires a group of experts to come together to focus on the design of a new product. For example, if you are working for a mobile telecommunications company, the brainstorming session should include all those involved in the design of the product (e.g. product marketing, usability experts, and design engineers). This should encourage a range of different ideas (motivated by the different perspectives each person brings to the brainstorming session). It is also important that no judgmental evaluations are made once ideas start getting generated as this could make people reticent about putting forward their creative solutions.

PROTOTYPING TECHNIQUES

If your research project is concerned with interface design issues, you will probably have to develop a prototype at some stage to help you test your hypothesis. In the real world of mobile product design, prototyping is used as part of the iterative design process. If you work as part of a design team (as an information architect or usability engineer) you may be asked to design a prototype of part of the system to assess its functionality in order to see if it should be included in the final product.

As mentioned earlier in this chapter, before you start to build your prototype you should have a clear picture of the tasks you expect your target users to carry out and how they will achieve these tasks. Once you have a clear idea of these scenarios and the steps needed for participants to complete them, then you are ready to start thinking about building your prototype.

When it comes to developing your mobile application prototypes there are two prototyping techniques at your disposal: paper and pencil testing and emulators. The aim of this section is to discuss each of these in turn.

Paper and pencil prototyping

One advantage of developing a paper and pencil prototype is that it is cheap and easy to use. Basically the idea behind this approach is that you put parts of the interface that you want to test on to card or paper. This can be achieved using drawing packages or using scaled drawings.

The first thing you have to do is to design the 'device'. This could be a paper-based version of the mobile phone handset interface, for example, that the participant in your study would interact with. Note: the screen space should be a bit larger than the one that would be used in real life, as handwriting takes up more space on the page than computer generated text.

Next, you will need to create a series of pages which will reflect the information that would appear on the screen at each stage of the user's interaction with the system. This will include menu lists, text entry fields, hyperlinks. You should also think about how you will represent user interface elements such as push buttons, softkeys, as well as how will you represent the 'cursor waiting' as you change from one screen page to another.

For an excellent step-by-step approach to creating paper prototypes, I recommend that you read Chapter 5 of Scott Weiss' (2002) book *Handheld Usability*.

Emulators

One of the major advantages that the online prototype has over the paper and pencil prototype is that it is a lot quicker to create! In an ideal world, the best way to test your prototype is on the actual handheld device that the service will be used with. However, as in a lot of student projects, you won't have the resources to do this. By way of compensation you can use a desktop emulator. For example, Openwave will allow you to develop your own mobile phone designs. Openwave is a freely available software development kit (see http://developer.openwave. com/dvl).

There are a few drawbacks that you should be aware of when you use a desktop emulator, as these could have an impact on the results of your study. Firstly, some people may think that it's really just another computer screen that they are interacting with, rather than a simulated mobile phone interface. Secondly, the input methods will not be realistic as the user may use the mouse and the keyboard to interact with the emulator. Finally, the appearance will obviously be different from the real device.

The main thing to do here is always to remind your user that it is a prototype that they are dealing with, not the real thing. You can also add functions to the prototype to make it look as real as possible such as *scroll up* and *scroll down* options, *text entry* options, etc.

You should also be aware of the speed in which information is updated on your screen, as this could have an impact on the user's perception of the usability of the system.

Wizard of Oz prototyping

The Wizard of Oz (WoZ) experimental scheme is a technique used for the simulation of interfaces that are currently partly built and may not be fully functional. The basic idea behind this technique is that a 'hidden' experimenter, the wizard, takes on some aspects of the role of the computer in a simulated human–computer interaction. The origin of the term is unknown but is commonly associated with F. Baum's (1990) book – *The Wizard of Oz*. This simulation technique is also sometimes referred to as the PNAMBIC (Pay No Attention to the Man BehInd the Curtain) technique. This technique is commonly used by mobile phone companies to test services that are currently at the development stage.

Fraser and Gilbert (1990) put forward three pre-conditions that must be satisfied before making a WoZ simulation useful:

1. It must be possible for the wizard to realistically simulate the computer system.
2. The designers of the system should have a clear understanding of the functionality of the future system before they try to simulate it.

3. The WoZ simulation should convey the illusion that the user is indeed interacting with a 'real' computer system. This is easier for some systems than others. For example, if the system only communicates to the user via text on the screen, the wizard can buffer the text to make sure that it appears on the screen one line at a time, rather than at the wizard's typing speed. For speech output systems things can be a bit more problematic. Fraser and Gilbert (1990) mention that it is important to disguise the wizard's speech to make it more mechanical (although I am not sure if that is a good idea) and the wizard must constrain their responses to those that match the system's capabilities. This could be easily achieved for systems that rely on dialogue prompts, but may be more difficult for systems that rely on more natural, conversational dialogue styles.

Fraser and Gilbert (1990) provide a partial taxonomy of WoZ simulations into those which use natural language modalities such speech and typing, and those which use modalities such as the manipulation of symbols in a GUI or keypad input.

They then go on to further sub-divide natural language simulations into two categories. One where only one of the parties in the interaction uses natural language (wizard or participant) and one where both participant and wizard interact using natural language. An example of where only the participant uses natural language is provided by Hauptmann (1989). In this study, the participant was asked to manipulate graphical images on a computer screen by issuing spoken commands to the computer. In turn, the wizard responded to these commands by typing instructions to the computer in order to manipulate the images in the way requested by the user. An example of a study whereby the wizard uses natural language and the user responds in a non-linguistic modality is provided by Labrador and Dinesh (1984). In this study, participants were asked to access a text messaging service using a telephone keypad and the system responded to these prompts by synthetic speech output.

Other categories of WoZ simulation using natural language are as follows:

1. The participant and the wizard are required to type.
2. The participant speaks and the wizard types.
3. The participant and the wizard speak.
4. The participant types and the wizard speaks.

An important factor to bear in mind if you are thinking of using this prototyping method is that the wizard must be thoroughly trained before you start your study. It is important not only that the wizard recognises the dialogue prompts, but also that the wizard is able to respond to commands from the user in an appropriate timescale (i.e. approximately the same time as you expect your future system to take). Overall, the WoZ approach, if implemented correctly, can be a very effective approach to adopt, especially if you are undertaking research looking at speech-based mobile phone services and applications.

SUMMARY

This chapter provided an overview of an HCD approach (ISO 13407) which is essential for the development of usable mobile applications and systems. The key stages of this approach were: understand and specify the context of use; specify the user and organisational requirements; produce designs and prototypes; and undertake user based assessment.

As part of this human-centred design approach, there was also a discussion on design principles that you should be aware of when developing a mobile system or application. An important point to consider from the outset is context of use. The context of use for a user of mobile applications is often highly dynamic with constantly changing social, physical and environmental influences. Therefore the suggestion put forward was that the designer should accommodate these, if possible, in the service or application design. Another key aspect to bear in mind when developing a mobile application or service is the limited screen space available on mobile devices; it is important that the designer reduces the information complexity without losing any valuable content. The discussion then moved on to focus on design issues for automated mobile phone services, with an emphasis being placed on how to reduce the burden on users' short-term memory.

Following on from this, the chapter provided an overview of requirements gathering techniques such as card sorting and brain storming that be used as part of a human-centred design approach to mobile product development. These techniques compliment other techniques on gathering information from users as discussed in Chapters 3 and 4 of this book.

A key aspect of mobile application design is the development of proto-types to evaluate initial design ideas and partially functional systems. Therefore, the last section of the chapter provided an overview of various prototyping techniques, such as paper and pencil prototyping and emulaters available on the internet, both of which can be used to develop prototypes for mobile devices.

Self test

- Wizard of Oz
- Emulators
- Metaphors
- Earcons
- Context of use
- Conversational dialogues
- Human-centred design
- Requirement gathering techniques

Exercises

1. Develop a new location-based mobile phone service for local authority services using openwave development.
2. Develop a speech-based mobile phone cinema information and booking service. Assess the usability of this service using a Wizard of Oz set-up.

REFERENCES

Barnard, E., Halberstadt, A. Kotelly, C. and Phillips, M. (1999) A consistent approach to designing spoken-dialogue systems. In *Proceedings of the Automatic Speech Recognition and Understanding Workshop*. Keystone, CO: USA

Baum, F. (1900) *The Wizard of Oz*. Collins, London

Blattner, M.M., Sumikawa, D.A. and Greenberg, R.M. (1989) Earcons and icons: their structure and common design principles. *Human–Computer Interaction*, 4(1), 11–44

Brewster, S.A. (1997) Navigating telephone-based interfaces with earcons. In *Proceedings of BCS HCI 1997*, Bristol, UK, pp. 39–56

Brewster, S.A. (2002) Overcoming the lack of screen space on mobile computers. *Personal and Ubiquitous Computing*, **6**, 188–205

Brewster, S.A. Raty, V.-P. and Kortekangas, A. (1996) Earcons as a Method of Providing Navigational Cues in a Menu Hierarchy. In *Proceedings of HCI '96* (Imperial College, London, UK), Springer, pp. 167–183

Brewster, S.A., Wright, P.C. & Edwards, A.D.N. (1993), cited in the text. In *An evaluation of earcons for use in auditory human-computer interfaces*. S. Ashlund, K. Mullet, A. Henderson, E. Hollnagel, and T. White (Eds.), Proceedings of InterCHI '93, Amsterdam: ACM Press, Addison-Wesley, pp. 222–227

Bristow, G. (1986) The speech recognition problem. In *Electric Speech Recognition*, Bristow, G. (Ed.), Collins

Fraser, N.M. and Gilbert, G.N. (1990) Simulating speech systems. *Computer Speech and Language*, **5**(1), 81–90

Hauptmann, A.G. (1989) Speech and gestures for graphic image manipulation. I, *Proceedings of CHI 1989*, Austin, Texas, USA, pp. 241–245

Howell, M.D., Love, S. and Turner, M. (2005) Spatial metaphors for a speech-based mobile city guide service. *Journal of Personal and Ubiquitous Computing*, **9**, 32–45

Labrador, C. and Dinesh, P. (1984) Experiments in speech interaction with conversational data services. In *Proceedings of INTERACT 1984*, London, UK, pp. 104–108

Leplatre, G. and Brewter, S.A. (2000) Designing non-speech sounds to support navigation in mobile phone menus. In *Proceedings of ICAD 2000*, Atlanta, USA, pp. 190–199

Maguire, M.C. (2001a) Methods to support human-centred design. *International Journal of Human–computer Studies*, **55**(4), 587–634

Maguire, M.C. (2001b) Context of use within usability activities. *International Journal of Human–computer Studies*, **55**, 453–483

Marcus, A. (2002) Metaphors and user interfaces in the 21st century. *Interactions*, **9**(2), 7–10

McDonald, J.E. and Schvaneveldt, R.W. (1988) The application of user knowledge to interface design. In *Cognitive Science and its Applications for Human–Computer Interaction*. R. Guindon (Ed.). Hillsadale: Lawrence Erlbaum, pp. 289–338

Noyes, J. (2001) Talking and writing – how natural in human-machine interaction? *International Journal of Human–Computer Studies*, **55**(4), 503–519

Osborn, A.F. (1963) *Applied imagination*. New York: Schribeners and Sons

Pirhonen, A., Brewster, S.A. and Holguin, C. (2002), Gestural and audio metaphors as a means of control for mobile devices. Proccedings of CHI 2002 (New York: ACM), pp. 291–298

Preece, J.J., Rogers, Y.R., Sharp, H., Benyon, D.R., Holland, S. and Carey, T. (1994) *Human–Computer Interaction*. Addison-Wesley

Preece, J.J., Rogers, Y.R. and Sharp, H. (2002) *Interaction Design: Beyond Human–Computer Interaction*. John Wiley and Sons

Rosenfeld, L. and Morville, P. (1998) *Information Architecture for the World Wide Web*. Cambridge: O'Reilly

Schmandt, C. (1987) Conversational telecommunications environments. In *Cognitive Engineering in the Design of Human–Computer Interaction and Expert Systems*, G. Salvendy, (Ed.). Elsevier Science

Smith, D.C., Irby, C., Kimball, R., Verplank, B. and Harslem, E. (1982) Designing the star user interface. *Byte*, **7**(4), 242–282

Souvignier, V., Kellner, A., Rueber, B., Schramm, H. and Seide, F. (2000) The thoughtful elephant: strategies for spoken dialogue systems. *IEEE Transactions of Speech and Audio Process*, **8**(1), 51–62.

Weiss, S. (2002) *Handheld Usability*. John Wiley and Sons

SUGGESTED FURTHER READING

Longoria, R. (Ed.) (2004) *Designing Software for the Mobile Context: A Practitioner's Guide*. Springer

Neilson, J. (1993) *Usability Engineering*. Cambridge, MA: Academic Press

Norman, D.A. (1999) *The Design of Everyday Things*, MIT Press

Pitt, I. and Edwards, A. (2003) *Design of Speech-based Devices*. Springer

6

Social usability

INTRODUCTION

This chapter focuses on the use of mobile devices, particularly when they are used in public places. There is a strong emphasis placed on mobile phone usage throughout the chapter, as the mobile phone, more than any other form of mobile device, is having the most significant impact on the way we behave in public places. Therefore the discussion will focus on the *social usability* of mobile devices. Social usability can be defined here as environmental and social factors; such as current locations, expectations, interpretations of behaviour, that influence people's own behaviour and attitude towards the use of mobile technology in social situations.

SOCIAL IMPACT OF MOBILE TECHNOLOGY

As the use of mobile telecommunications increases (particularly that of mobile phones) there is a growing body of research that indicates that use of mobile communications are influencing how we go about our daily lives from both a social and economic perspective. According to a study carried about by Wei and Leung (1999), the majority of calls being made by mobile phone users takes place on streets, on public transport, in shops and in restaurants. This finding will probably not surprise you as you will be used to seeing people using mobile phones on trains, in cafés and restaurants, etc. In addition, you have probably (unintentionally, of course) heard the topics of some of these conversations, which may have been business orientated (e.g. someone talking to a client) or more socially orientated (e.g. arranging to meet a friend to go to the cinema).

What is the social impact of these forms of mobile communication? Let's have a look at the research literature.

Public performance

Mobile phones now occupy concurrent social spaces, spaces with norms (behaviour standards that members of the social group are expected to conform to, by others in the social group) that sometimes conflict; such as the space of the mobile phone user, and the virtual space where the conversation takes place (Palen *et al.*, 2000). This has resulted in a lively public debate about what is acceptable and unacceptable in relation to mobile phone use in public places.

An example of this conflict is provided by Ling (2002) in a study he carried out while investigating the social impact of mobile phone use in public places. In this study he found that people perceived mobile phone use in places such as restaurants as unacceptable. This was partly because people tend to talk louder than usual when using mobile phones and as a result of this, individuals located near mobile phone users felt coerced into eavesdropping into their conversation. This seems to suggest that people believe there should be some form of 'mobile etiquette', for the use of mobile phones in public places. This is not so far fetched as you may think. For example, mobile phone companies are issuing guidelines on 'mobile etiquette' encouraging sensible and responsible mobile phone behaviour in public places (BT Cellnet, 2001). In addition, some train companies (in the UK) now have 'quiet carriages' where mobile phones have to be on silent mode and anyone wishing to make or receive a mobile phone call is requested to go to the end of the carriage so as not to disturb the other passengers. The idea of a 'quiet carriage' has also been adopted by train companies in Norway and Japan. I am sure you can think of experiences you have had when someone sitting next to you on the train have started what you perceive to be a loud, long and unnecessary conversation. You may feel annoyed that you cannot concentrate on reading your book. Alternatively, you may wish you could hear what the other person is saying because the conversation sounds interesting! However, have you ever thought about the social impact on other people when it is you who is making the mobile phone call on the train?

Continuing with mobile phone behaviour on trains, Murtagh (2000) presented findings from an observational study of the non-verbal aspects of mobile phone use in a train carriage. Murtagh found that changing the direction of one's gaze, turning one's head and upper body away from the other people sitting next to them in the carriage was a common feature of mobile phone behaviour on trains. These behavioural responses were seen as being indicative of the subtle complexities involved in using mobile phones in public locations.

In terms of a theoretical perspective, the work of Murtagh, Ling, and Palen and co-workers, have all been influenced by the work of Erving Goffman. In his book entitled *The Presentation of Self in Everyday Life* (1959), Goffman suggested that people have specific 'public faces' and personas for different social locations. For Goffman, the central issue was to describe the situations that individuals were in and not to describe the individuals themselves. The idea behind this is that individuals have rules that determine their behaviour in public places, or what Burns (1992) refers to as the 'observance of social propriety'. For example, you would expect your bank manager to be calm and sober, and talk about your financial situation in a conscientious way. How would you feel if he talked about your finances in a more extraverted manner, wandering about his office, and making jokes about your financial predicament?

One can see the relevance of Goffman's theory when considering Murtagh's study. Goffman also talks about 'civil inattention' in public places and when a person engages in a mobile phone conversation on a train, other individuals in close proximity may be drawn, unwillingly ('coerced into eavesdropping' to use Goffman's terms), into what is essentially a private conversation. In this case it is the mobile phone user who is being civilly inattentive to the people around them. Therefore, it can be said that the mobile phone medium interacts with the social status quo and individuals change their behaviour as a result of this.

Ethnography

In terms of research design methodology, the underlying approach to a lot of the work carried out in this area has been ethnographic. What is ethnographic research? According to Atkinson and Hammersley (1994) the main features of ethnographic research are as follows:

- You should have a clear idea of the particular social phenomena you are interested in observing (e.g. people's reaction to mobile phone use in public places).
- Focus on a small number of users (usually).
- Analysis will be based on describing and explaining the human actions you have observed in a particular social context (e.g. observing people's reaction to mobile phone conversations going on next to them in a restaurant).
- The role of statistical analysis is minor.

One can see from the research outlined above how this methodological approach has been very successful in helping researchers to investigate the social impact of mobile phone use in public places. However, there is another perspective that we can adopt to investigate this phenomenon.

Psychological perspective

Research into the interaction between an individual and a given situation has been well-documented in Psychology. For example, Argyle *et al.* (1981), looked at the personality-situation interaction and found that personality traits such as extraversion and introversion had an impact on how individuals would behave in particular situations. They reported that introverts, for example, would use avoidance behaviour in order to get out of a situation they would find (or would potentially find) uncomfortable. This implies that there is some form of social perception taking place on the part of the individual. This social perception is also known as a 'social schema'. Fiske (1995) defines a social schema as a guide for individuals to gauge their feelings, thoughts and actions in social situations. For example, you arrange to meet a friend in a café and when she then goes on to behave in a way that contradicts your expectations of her behaviour in this situation, you could say that your social schema for this situation is being challenged. However, Fiske also states that people are 'cognitive misers' in that we try to keep our social schemas in order to preserve a reality that fits our own expectations of a particular social situation.

This clearly is an important factor to consider when it comes to explaining the attitudes (and behaviours) of individuals towards mobile phone use in public places. Is the reason why we get annoyed with mobile phone conversations in places such as restaurants, train carriages, etc., due to the social schema we have for that social situation? Our social schema for behaviour may tell us that it is wrong for us to have mobile phone conversations in restaurants because it is rude or impolite, especially if our lunch guest is sitting there waiting for us while we make our call. However, the question that needs to be asked here is: are we just being a 'cognitive miser' in this situation? If so, will our social schema for this type of situation change over time as more and more people (including ourselves) start to make and receive mobile phone calls in restaurants? Another interesting aspect to this situation could be the attitude of the restaurant management. In order to not lose any customers, they might decide that there should be mobile phone-free areas in their restaurant, just like some train companies now have mobile phone-free carriages.

Another factor that is relevant to observing and trying to understand peoples' behaviour in social situations is the issue of interpersonal space. The majority of studies investigating interpersonal space issues have been carried out in public places such as shops, libraries, and workplaces. For example, Wollman *et al.* (1994) focused their study on the intrusion of an individual's personal space in the workplace. Others, such as Veitch and Arkkelin (1995), investigated the relationship between individuals who did not know each other.

One major underlying factor emerging from this work has been the idea of an individual feeling crowded when they perceive their personal space to have been invaded. Sears *et al.* (1988) define crowding as a feeling of discomfort, and stress related to spatial aspects of the environment that an individual is currently in. The idea of personal space being related to some measurement of interpersonal distance can be traced back to the work of Hall (1966).

Hall stated that personal space could be divided into a series of zones:

- *Intimate zone*: a distance of up to 45 cm from the individual. Only close relatives or close friends are normally allowed into this zone (e.g. girlfriend or boyfriend).
- *Personal zone*: a distance of up to 1.2 m from the individual. Usually family and friends are allowed in this zone.
- *Social zone*: a distance between about 1 m and 3 m from the individual. An example of the social zone is the typical space between work colleagues who are engaged in conversation.

- **Public zone**: a distance between about 3 m and 8 m from the individual. An example of the public zone is a lecturer delivering a lecture to a group of students in a lecture theatre.

There are, however, several factors that can have an affect on the inter-personal distance preferred by individuals. Firstly, there is the cross-cultural dimension. Shortly after Hall published his work, Watson and Graves (1966) published an account of the difference in personal space preferred between individuals from America and some Mediterranean countries (who preferred a shorter distance between the speakers) when it came to having a normal conversation. A violation of this space by either party led to a feeling of discomfort by the other. Personal char-acteristics can also have an impact. Studies have suggested that females interacting with other females tend to have a smaller distance between them than males interacting with other males (Gifford, 1987). In add-ition, Kaya and Erkíp (1999) suggested that females prefer a greater distance between themselves and males.

Another important factor in determining interpersonal distance is the situation that the interaction takes place in. For example, in high-density situations (e.g. travelling on an increasingly crowded underground train) people can experience feelings of discomfort. In situations like this, limited physical resources have to be shared between greater numbers of people and, at the same time, there is a concomitant increase in phys-ical contact between individuals that can lead to a decrease in the indi-vidual's feelings of privacy. As a result of situations like this Hall (1966) reported that people tend to experience more negative feelings towards others in high-density situations than in other lower density situations. For example, if you are travelling on the underground system in London *tube etiquette* requires you to try and studiously avoid making any kind of eye contact with any individual who is about 2 cm from you in the tube carriage during rush hour. Also, trying to strike up any kind of con-versation with anyone will result in the individual adopting the pose (if there's room in the carriage) and expression of a rabbit being caught in the beam from the headlights of a car.

Taking the interaction between the individual and the situation as a starting point, I carried out an experiment (Love, 2001) to investigate the idea that participants perceived themselves being drawn, short-term, into the personal zone of an individual who engaged in a mobile phone conversation while seated in a waiting room. The study also explored whether or not this was dependent on the perceived nature of the conversation, e.g. private (a telephone call from the bank regarding an overdraft request) or social (arranging to meet a friend for a drink).

People taking part in the study were asked to wait in a waiting room while I got the experiment ready. The other person in the room was, in fact, an actor. After I left the room again, I phoned the actor on his mobile phone. He proceeded to either have a conversation with the bank or his friend. I observed the situation from behind a two-way mirror. When the mobile phone conversation finished (after about a minute or so) I came in and explained the nature of the real study and asked participants a few questions. I found that some people felt they were drawn unwillingly into listening to the conversation as they were sitting so close to the individual having the mobile phone conversation. Other people were quite happy to listen in, to invade the personal space of the person having the mobile phone call as it were. As one participant memorably told me: '*I can tell you every word of the conversation as I was listening intently to it*'. Overall, I found that people were split into two groups: those who felt they were drawn unwillingly into the virtual space of the mobile phone conversation, and those who didn't feel drawn into the virtual personal space of the people involved in the mobile phone call. In order to explore the reasons for this, I carried out another study to investigate whether or not personality had anything to do with these feelings (Love and Kewley, 2005). The results from this study indicate that personality characteristics such as introversion and extraversion do have an affect on people's perception of mobile phone use in public places.

Having primarily been focusing on inter-personal relations so far, let's consider another context of mobile phone use: the mobile worker.

Mobile workers

Perry *et al.* (2001) define a mobile worker as somebody who works in different locations (e.g. a district nurse making home visits); someone working in one specific location but walking around whilst they are there (e.g. architect working on-site); someone working when they are travelling between locations (e.g. salesman on the train between visiting two clients updating his files on his laptop).

If you look at each of these situations in turn, you will quickly come to realise that as mobile workers inhabit dynamic environments, they have different demands in terms of the resources that are needed for mobile communication and the constraints that impede mobile communication. For example, if you are working on the train, how reliable is the WiFi connection in the carriage you are working in? However, what I want to focus on in this section are the social dynamics of being a mobile worker.

According to Kraut (2003) effective communication is probably the most important group interaction. Why? Because people can co-ordinate their contributions to specific tasks, and people can also call on the expertise of others in the group or organisation to help them solve a particular problem, or contribute to a project that they have in hand.

In the research literature in the area of CSCW, an interesting area of research to emerge has been the community of practice (CoP) which looks at groupings of individuals in a work environment. According to Wenger (1999), the activities people carry out at work can occur in either one CoP or several CoPs. These groups emerge over time and basically people come together to share what they've learned in their jobs that may be of benefit to others working in similar areas. In one of the most well-known studies of this phenomenon, Orr (1996) studied the CoP of repair technicians at Xerox. It was found that through telling each other how they had fixed tricky problems with troublesome copy machines, they were able to collectively improve the company's efficiency in repairing copy machines when they were called out on jobs. So much so, that they were subsequently given mobile devices to be able to communicate with each other even more after the results of the study were published!

A key factor in having a successful CoP is *awareness*. Dourish and Belloti (1992) define awareness as 'an understanding of the activities of others, which provides a context for your own activity'. How can you do this when you are mobile? Wiberg and Ljunberg (2000) found that being aware of other colleagues' activities can be problematic when you are mobile. For example, in their study, they found that the engineers they spoke to worked alone, and often found it difficult to keep up-to-date with developments in other engineers projects. In another study, Laurier (2001) found that mobile workers tried to get round this awareness problem by using their mobile phones to keep in contact with others. They were able to team build, and tried to create a concept of a mobile office by adopting the convention of switching off their phones when they were in a meeting to mimic the 'meeting in progress' sign they would have put on the door of their office back at work.

From what we have discussed above, it is clear that this is an area that will need further investigation as the numbers of mobile workers increases. The challenge for researchers and designers of mobile applications and devices is to consider who are the mobile workers, and the dynamic context in which the use these devices (e.g. not only on location). In addition, more research will need to be undertaken to investigate the social impact on being a mobile worker.

SUMMARY

The aim of this chapter was to investigate the social impact of mobile technology, with particular focus on mobile phones. The chapter has shown that there is an emerging body of research that indicates that mobile phone use is having a social impact (not always perceived as positive) on our behaviour, and attitudes towards mobile phone use in public places.

The chapter also provided examples of how this question has been approached from a research design perspective. For example, the two studies outlined above indicate how one could carry out a research project that addresses specific aspects of individuals interacting with mobile technology in the social environment (e.g. the affects of personality). In addition, we also saw how there is a strong *Sociological* dimension to this area of work as well as a *Psychological* one.

When considering the social and concomitant environmental influences that affect the use of mobile devices in public locations, it is necessary to consider what factors contribute to each of these.

Environment: the location you are in; the technology you have your disposal.

Social: social norms for the situation you are in (i.e. you have expectations of what is considered normal behaviour in this situation, while other people have expectations of what is considered normal/acceptable behaviour in this situation), personal space, cultural differences.

Meyrowitz (1985) talked about how electronic media affected social behaviour by reorganising social settings and altering the relationship between the physical place and the social place. The results from these studies fit in with this perspective as they indicate that individuals have to think about (and perhaps in the long-term, reorganise) their social schemas for public situations such as sitting in a waiting room, when mobile phone use is involved. For example, in one study that we have looked at here, some individuals clearly felt uncomfortable being close to someone having a mobile phone conversation, and they tried to look for ways to change their own behaviour to make them more feel comfortable. However, other individuals did not feel uncomfortable in this situation as they felt that it was ok for people to have mobile phone conversations in waiting rooms. The results from this study also suggested that personality, perhaps, could have an impact on the social schemas that individuals were creating for mobile phone use in public places such as the waiting room. The affect of personality on peoples' attitudes towards mobile phone use in public places was, therefore, explored in study two. The results obtained from the second study indicate that personality does have an impact on peoples' attitudes towards mobile phone use in public places, especially if one is in close proximity to the person making or receiving a mobile phone call.

There are, however, other aspects that may be worth considering here in relation to the social impact of mobile technology. For example, an interesting addition to this body of work would be an investigation into any cross-cultural differences on mobile phone use in public places. One piece of anecdotal evidence provides an example of this. In Singapore, it is not uncommon for people to 'cup' their hand round the mouthpiece of their mobile phone when they are speaking into it in public places. What is the significance of this type of behaviour? When asked for an explanation, several people indicated that they thought that it was polite (i.e. more socially acceptable) to be as unobtrusive as possible when making a mobile phone call in a public place. Will this type of behaviour change over time?

Cross-cultural research into the design and use of mobile applications should also be of interest to mobile telecommunication companies working on a global scale. It is important to consider the importance of cross-cultural behaviour, in the design of their information systems, in this instance mobile informatics.

To conclude this section, looking at the broader perspective, the research reported here can be seen as part of a growing volume of multi-disciplinary empirical work that seeks to investigate the role of technology in relation to the changing perception of social space (Cooper, 2000). There is however, the need for further research in this area. Potential areas for research are discussed in Chapter 9.

Self test

- Civil inattention
- Ethnography
- Social schema
- Social usability

Exercises

1. Design a Likert attitude scale that you could give to a group of people in order to find out their attitudes towards mobile phone use on the train.

2. The next time you are in a restaurant or café watch the reactions of people who are in close proximity to someone who either receives or makes a call on their mobile phone. How would classify their reactions?

3. What other personal characteristics, apart from personality, do you think could have an affect on peoples' behaviour and attitudes towards mobile phone use in public places?

REFERENCES

Argyle, M., Furnham, A. and Graham, J.A. (1981) *Social Situations.* Cambridge University Press.

BT Cellnet (2001) Mobile Etiquette: Changing the way we use our mobiles. http://www.btcellnet.net/cgi-bin accessed 15/10/01.

Atkinson, P. and Hammersley, M. (1994) Ethnography and Participant Observation. In *Handbook of Qualitative Research*, N. Denzin and Lincoln (Eds.), Sage: Thousand Oaks, pp. 249–261

Burns, T. (1992) *Erving Goffman.* London: Routledge

Cooper, G. (2000) The mutable world: social theory in the wireless world. In *Wireless World: Social and Interactional Aspects of the Mobile Age,* Brown, B., Green, N. and Harper, R. (Eds.). Springer

Fiske, S. (1995) Social Cognition. In *Advanced Social Psychology*, Tesser, A. (Ed.). pp. 149–194. New York: McGraw-Hill

Gifford, R. (1987) *Environmental Psychology: Principles and Practice.* Boston: Allyn

Goffman, E. (1959) *The Presentation of Self in Everyday Life.* New York: Doubleday

Hall, E.T. (1966) *The Hidden Dimension: Man's Use of Space in Public and Private.* Bodley Head: London

Harper, R., Randall, D. and Rouncefield, M. (2000) *Organisational Change and Retail Finance: An Ethnographic Perspective.* London: Routeledge

Kaya, N. and Erkíp, F. (1999) Invasion of personal space under the condition of short-term crowding: a case study on an automatic teller machine. *Journal of Environmental Psychology,* **19**, 183–189

Laurier, E. (2001) Why people say where they are during mobile phone calls. Environmental and Planning D: Society and Space, **19**, 485–504

Ling, R. (2002) 'The social juxtaposition of mobile telephone conversations and public spaces'. In *The Social Consequences of Mobile Telephones,* Kim, S.D. (Ed.), Chunchon, Korea

Love, S. (2001) 'Space Invaders: Do Mobile Phone Conversations Invade Peoples' Personal Space?' *Proceedings of the 18th International Human Factors in Telecommunications Symposium in Bergen, Norway,* 5–7 November 2001, pp. 125–131

Love, S. and Kewley, J. (in press) *The Affects of Personality on People's Attitude Towards Mobile Phone Conversations in Public Places, Mobile Communications: Re-Negotiation of the Social Sphere,* Ling, R. and Pederson, P. (Eds.), Springer-Verlag

Meyrowitz, J. (1985) *No Sense of Place: The Impact of Electronic Media on Social Behaviour.* Oxford University Press

Murtagh, G. (2000) Seeing the 'Rules': Preliminary observations of action, interaction and mobile phone use. In *Wirless World: Social and Interactional Aspects of the Mobile Age,* Brown, B., Green, N. and Harper, R. (Eds.). London: Springer

Palen, L., Salzman, M. and Youngs, E. (2000) Going Wireless: behaviour and practice of new mobile phune Users. In *Proceeding of the ACM 2000 Conference on Computer Supported Cooperative Work,* Philadelphia, PA, pp. 201–210. New York: ACM Press

Sears, O.D., Peplau, A. and Freedman, J. (1988) *Social Psychology.* New York: Prentice Hall

Veitch, R. and Arkkelin, D. (1995) *Environmental Psychology: An Interdisciplinary Perspective,* New York: Prentice Hall

Watson, O.M. and Graves, T.D. (1966) Quantitative research in proxemic behaviour. *American Anthropology,* **68**, 971–985. Cited in Eysenck, M.W. (2000) *Psychology: A Student's Handbook,* The Psychology Press Ltd

Wei, R. and Leung, L. (1999) Blurring public and private behaviours in public space: policy challenges in the use and improper use of the cell phone. *Telematics and Informatics,* **16**, 11–26

Wollman, N., Kelly, B.M. and Bordens, K.S. (1994) Environmental and intrapersonal predictors of reactions to potential territorial intrusions in the workplace. *Environment and Behaviour,* **26**, 179–194

SUGGESTED FURTHER READING

Ager, J. (2003) *In Constant Touch: a global history of the mobile telephone.* Icon books, UK

Katz, J. and Aarkhus, M. (Eds.) (2002) *Perpetual Contact: mobile communication, private talk, public performance.* Cambridge University Press, UK

Ling, R. (2004) *The Mobile Connection: the cell phone's impact on society.* Morgan Kaufmann, San Francisco, CA

Rheingold, H. (2002) *Smart Mobs: the next social revolution.* Perseus Book Group, Cambridge, MA

7

Research guidelines for projects

INTRODUCTION

This chapter focuses on providing you with guidelines for starting your own mobile HCI project. Specifically, this chapter provides you with information on how to get started on a literature search; how to get focused on your aims and objectives; tips on project management; and how to choose the appropriate methods for your study. In addition, it provides you with information on how to write up your mobile HCI project.

CHOOSING A TOPIC FOR STUDY

When it comes to undertaking your research study you may be given a specific topic to research but most of the time you will probably be expected to come up with your own idea for a research topic. The key thing to remember from the outset is that when it comes to choosing a topic for study, it's important that you make an *informed decision*.

How can you go about this? There are a number of ways. In the first instance, you may think back to your lectures (if you can remember any of them) and think about something interesting that was covered in a lecture (again this could be problematic). Next, follow-up the references related to the topic, if any were given at the end of the lecture. You could even make an appointment to see the lecturer to discuss your research ideas in more detail. In which case, it might help if you write some ideas down on paper before your appointment so that you can use your meeting effectively.

You can also perhaps look over past projects that have been carried out by students in your department. Although you won't be able to undertake exactly the same project, you may get a few ideas about a topic you can look at.

Literature search

Getting hold of references to read is an essential part of the background preparatory work for your study. By reading the research literature on your proposed area of study you can clarify the direction your own project will take. For example, you may get ideas on how you can con-duct your study (e.g. what evaluation methods to use), you could also find out what did and did not work in terms of a research approach for others. In addition, you could identify a gap in the research literature which will give you the opportunity to carry out a project from a more novel perspective.

In order to conduct a literature review, you need to find out what types of resources you have available you. According to Sharp *et al.* (2002), categories of resources that a researcher has available are *primary* and *secondary* resources. Here are some examples of what they mean by this.

Primary sources include the following:

- Academic journal articles (e.g. International Journal of Human–computer Studies, Personal and Ubiquitous Computing)
- Conference proceedings (e.g. Mobile HCI, CHI, UbiComp)
- Codes of Practice (e.g. British Computer Society, ACM, IEE, IEEE)
- Thesis and dissertations (e.g. PhD thesis. These can be ordered through the inter-library loans system)
- Standards (e.g. ISO, ITU).

Secondary sources include the following:

- Textbooks (e.g. Dix, A. Finlay, J. , Abowd, G. and Beale, R. (2004) *Human–computer Interaction*, 3rd edition, Prentice Hall)
- Bulletin boards (e.g. Jakob Nielsen's alert box)

- Electronic resources such as ACM Digital Library (http://www.acm. org/dl/). You should note that you may need to get a password before you can access these types of resources.

Most people carry out their literature review searches electronically. However, to get the most from these electronic resources you have to think carefully about what you are going to search for before starting. This is where using Boolean Logic effectively can be a real time saver for you. When generating your search statements it's important to define the key words relating to the topic, think about the use of synonyms, check your spelling and use your Boolean operators (AND, OR, NOT) effectively. In order to illustrate this point, let's work through an example together.

Technical Tip 1

Generating literature search statements

Suppose my proposed research topic is in the general area of evaluating the usability of location-based mobile phone services. The first thing I must do is to decide on the key words that I should use in my search. In addition, I should also think about how far back in time I could go to get information. If I go too far back, I might get hold of information that is out of date – although with location-based service research this is highly unlikely at present. In addition, if you don't look back far enough you might miss what are known as '*seminal papers*'. That is, key references for the area that you are interested in studying. For this example, I think the key words are: mobile, HCI, usability, evaluation and services.

For the next step, I would access a search engine or an online electronic library and I would then use the following Boolean searches to help me find information on this topic:

Mobile AND HCI AND ('evaluation' OR 'usability study' AND 'service' OR 'location-based services').

Hopefully, by using search statements like that I will find considerable information to help me progress with my background exploration of my potential research study topic. One thing to mention here is that it is very important that you can keep track of all the references you come across and use in your literature review. Fortunately there are software packages available to help you create your own database of references, for example Microsoft's EndNote.

Project description

After you have reviewed the literature, you should be in a position to describe the aims and objectives for your study. It is important that you have a clear project aim (e.g. to investigate the effect of age on people's perception of the usability of an automated music catalogue service) and list the objectives that will allow you to investigate this. Your list will include factors such as:

- carry out a more comprehensive review of the literature in your chosen area of study.
- conduct a requirements gathering exercise with an appropriate sample of participants.
- develop a prototype based on the data obtained from the requirements gathering exercise.
- evaluate the prototype by getting participants to perform certain tasks and assess their performance and attitude towards the prototype.
- Write-up project report.

Choosing appropriate methods for your study

The aims of your study should determine the types of research methods that you choose to use in your study. As you will remember from Chapters 4 and 5, there are a number of methods and techniques that are available to you when carrying out mobile HCI projects. To refresh your memory, these are summarised in in Table 7.1.

Using my example for a potential research project, I would need to choose the appropriate methods and prototype design approach for the following stages of my project.

Requirements gathering

If you are interested in getting different perceptions of the usability of an automated catalogue service from different age groups, how will you find this out? Do you interview them? Or give them a questionnaire, observe them using the service, and then ask them questions afterwards? How will you get participants for this? For information of the techniques you could use here you can look back at Chapter 5, which gave you an introduction to generic research methods that can be used in mobile HCI research.

Table 7.1 Mobile HCI Research Methods and Techniques

Purpose of Study	Design Method	Strengths	Weaknesses	Associated Methods
System or service design	Lab based	Easy to collect data Easy for others to replicate your study	Artificial setting Can findings be generalised?	Observation Interviews Performance measures Heuristic evaluation Cognitive walkthrough
	Field study	Context of use Rich source of data	Time consuming to collect data Hard to replicate your study	Observation Interviews Survey
	Case Study	Context of use Rich source of data from a specific group of users	Time consuming to collect data Hard to replicate your study	Observation Interviews Survey Performance measures[1]
System or service evaluation	Lab based	Easy to collect data Easy for others to replicate your study	Artificial setting Can findings be generalised?	Observation Interviews Performance measures[1] Heuristic evaluation Cognitive walkthrough

(continued)

Table 7.1   (*continued*)

Purpose of Study	Design Method	Strengths	Weaknesses	Associated Methods
System or service evaluation (*contd*)	Field study	Context of use Rich source of data	Time consuming to collect data Hard to replicate your study	Observation Interviews Survey
	Case Study	Context of use Rich source of data from a specific group of users	Time consuming to collect data Hard to replicate your study	Observation Interviews Survey Performance measures[1]
Assessing impact of mobile ICT's	Field study or ethnographic study	Context of use Rich source of data	Time consuming to collect data Hard to replicate your study	Observation Interviews Survey
	Case Study	Context of use Rich source of data from a specific group of users	Time consuming to collect data Hard to replicate your study	Observation Interviews Survey

[1] For example, time to complete tasks, error rates.

Prototype design methods

After you have conducted the initial data collection phase you may want to develop a prototype of the service that meets the different usability needs of people of different ages. How will you go about this? Will you use an online emulator, or a paper and pencil prototype design? To refresh you memory on prototype evaluation techniques for mobile devices and applications, you could look at Chapter 5. Remember you have to justify your choices.

Evaluation methods

Once you have developed your prototype the next step is for you to evaluate it. How will you go about this? Will you get people to carry out specific tasks and take performance measures such as task completion? Will you collect information on their attitude towards the prototype (e.g. questionnaire, interview)? Will you use the same participants as before or will you try and recruit new ones? If you look back to Chapters 3 and 4, which deal with generic research methods and specific HCI research methods, you should be able to develop a set of measures that will allow you to evaluate the prototype system that you have developed. The key thing to remember is that the methods you propose to use should reflect the aims and objectives that you have specified for your study.

Project plan

At this stage it may also be a good idea to produce a project outline plan. This should include a breakdown of all the tasks you will have to undertake to achieve your project aims, as well as how long you expect each of these tasks to take. This should include information such as: how long you expect your literature review to take; how long you plan to spend on prototype development; how long you plan to spend on evaluation. In addition, you should also include timings on your actual project write-up.

Once you have written up this initial proposal you could send it to your supervisor and then arrange to see them to go over it. Remember to give your supervisor enough time to read over it and meet up with you to discuss it.

Project management

When you undertake your research project, you are in fact becoming a project manager. What do you need to do in order to manage your project? You need a project workplan, which we discussed in the previous section. However, in order to implement a good project plan you need to address two key issues:

1. Estimate how long it will take you to achieve milestones (i.e. complete the literature review) in your project.
2. Identify any potential risks associated with your project and ways in which you will deal with these.

When it comes to estimating timescales you have to consider factors such as:

1. How long will it take you to develop your prototype (especially if you have not used the prototype design method before)?
2. Have you undertaken a research project like this before? If not, what do other people think of your proposed timescales for doing things? Again talk to your friends and supervisor about this.
3. How long will it take you to read all the papers that you have painstakingly collected for your literature review?
4. How long will it take you to get an appropriate sample of participants to take part in your study?
5. How long will it take you to develop the data collection tools for your study (e.g. questionnaire, observation coding sheet, etc)?
6. How long will it take your supervisor to read a draft of your work? (Tip: do not give it to them the day before a deadline and expect feedback.)
7. When are the deadlines for handing in work associated with your project?
8. Should you include project meetings with your supervisor in your workplan?

In order to identify and manage risk in relation to your project you have to ask yourself these sorts of questions:

1. Does any part of the project depend on people or factors that are beyond your control? For example, getting participants to take part in your user study, ordering software or video recording equipment, or getting access to the HCI lab to carry out your study.
2. Are there parts of your project that are tricky to carry out? For example, developing a PDA prototype in order to test your hypothesis.

Once you have identified any potential risks the next step is to look for ways to manage these risks. This can include tackling the 'potential problem' parts of your project as early as possible. For example, developing a PDA prototype that will be used in your study. In addition, you should always have a contingency plan in case things go wrong with your project. This should include allocating time for this in your overall project plan and also having a 'Plan B' to allow you to reduce the size and scope of your project.

Problems with your project

Despite all your good efforts, there are times when things do start to go wrong with your project. So what should you do? Well, the first thing to do is not to panic (which I know may be difficult, if the deadline for your project is approaching fast). Stop and think:

1. What do you need to do to get back on track (e.g. should you reassess how long it will take you to carry out your evaluation and data analysis)?
2. Can your supervisor help you? (Hopefully the answer will be yes to this question.)
3. Do you have a back-up plan, if not how long will it take you to get one organised?

Ethical HCI research

An important aspect that is often overlooked in HCI research is the question of ethics.

The area of mobile HCI (and HCI in general) is driven by developments in technology and therefore is constantly changing and presenting new ethical challenges to designers and researchers alike. As it is a multidisciplinary research area, it has the opportunity of drawing on the codes of ethical practice from some of its constituent members. Members include: the Association of Computing Machinery (ACM), the British Psychological Society (BPS) and the American Psychological Association (APA).

However, students often overlook ethical considerations when carrying out HCI research. Many students are unaware of the fact that there are ethical considerations for them to address in the planning and carrying out of their HCI research projects.

Cairns and Thimbleby (2002) talk about the importance of HCI having 'best practice' procedures as in other disciplines such as medicine. So what are the best practice procedures that researchers in mobile HCI should be aware of? When you are preparing to conduct mobile HCI research you need to ask yourself the following sorts of questions that address the ethical implications of the work you are about to undertake:

1. Have you really thought about the tasks that you are asking your participants to undertake as part of your study? For example, is it ok to ask them to find 10 pieces of information using a PDA application, even though it takes an hour to do the test? Are you putting undue pressure on people to participate in the study?
2. Do you really need the personal information you asked participants to provide (e.g. age, gender and occupation)? How will this information help you achieve your research aims?
3. Have you informed participants what your study is about? Have you told them what will happen to their data? Have you told them how they can contact you afterwards to find out the results of the study? You should produce an informed consent form for your participants to read before they take part in your study – this will allow your participants to know what the study is about before taking part. This will help many of the ethical considerations in this list. Please see the Technical Tip 2 below for an example of an informed consent form.
4. Have you built in time to debrief participants taking part in your study? If participants have been deceived in any way (e.g. not made fully aware that their behaviour was being video taped), it is important that they are reassured and an explanation for any deception is given. For example, you may be interested in observing people's behaviour when they are in a public place and someone uses their mobile phone. You could set up an experiment whereby a participant comes into a waiting room with hidden cameras expecting to take part in an HCI study all about website navigation. Also present in the room could be another person waiting to take part in the study. Suddenly this other person (an actor) receives a mobile phone call. This other person could in fact be a collaborator of the experimenter's, helping out in the study. Once the deception has been explained, the participant should be asked if their data can still be used in your analysis.
5. If it is observational data you are collecting (video or note taking), should you tell the people that you have been observing them before or afterwards and get their consent to use the data?
6. Reporting results – have you presented all the results, including those that go against the aims of the study? Have you presented the findings objectively without resorting to any form of 'spin'?

Therefore, if you are conducting any form of HCI research, from a final year undergraduate dissertation project, to research for a new mobile telecommunications company or service, it is important that the participants who take part in your study are aware of what is going to happen to them during the study.

Technical Tip 2

Informed consent form

You should always try and gain informed consent from the people who take part in your studies. Obviously there are times when one is conducting mobile HCI research that obtaining prior permission could be problematic (e.g. observing naturally occurring behaviour in relation to mobile phones use in a café). However, if at all possible you should try and get the consent of the people who wittingly or unwittingly took part in your study.

The type of information that you should provide and the formal layout of the informed consent form could be similar to Figure 7.1.

My name is .... and I work in the School of Information Systems, Computing and Mathematics at Brunel University, West London, UK.

The aim of this study is to investigate people's perception of a speech-based cinema information service for mobile phones.

As part of this investigation you will be asked to find out the starting times for three films. After completing these tasks I will ask you to complete a short questionnaire that has been designed to obtain information about what you thought of the service.

All the data collected for this work will be presented in future publications anonymously. If you would like information on the findings of this study please leave me your contact details at the end and I will send you information on the results.

You can withdraw from the study at any time. If you have questions relating to the study please do not hesitate to ask me. Finally, I would like to thank you for agreeing to take part in my research project.

I have read the above statement and I am aware of my rights and responsibilities

Participant Name: ....
Date: ....

Figure 7.1   An Informed Consent Form

Analysis of data

Once you have selected the methods that you will use to carry out your study, you need to ascertain how you will analyse the data that you collect. One thing to remember at this stage is to always keep in mind your original aims and objectives when it comes to your data analysis. There are many powerful statistical packages available to used such as the Statistical Package for the Social Sciences (SPSS). Make sure you are familiar with how these work before you attempt to use them to analyse your data, perhaps by enrolling on a training course for the statistical package you want to use. Another important thing to remember is that you may need longer to analyse and interpret your data than you first envisaged. This is why it's always useful (as I mentioned in the project management section) that you give yourself a lot of scope here when it comes to planning this part of your project.

For a comprehensive review of the data analysis techniques that can be used for the data collected using the research methods (see Chapters 3 and 4), I suggest that you refer to Coolican (2000).

Writing up your report

Once you have carried out your study, collected the data and analysed it, the last thing you have to do is write up your project. Your supervisor will usually have guidelines for the format of the report. For example, if it is a final-year project report, your department probably will have provided you with information regarding the margin sizes, font size, word length, and guidance on the structure of your report. It is important that you are very clear on what the report should contain and how it should be formatted before you start your write-up.

Tips on report writing

What follows is an example of what the structure and content of a final year undergraduate mobile HCI project may look like.

Title

The title should not be too long. Be as concise as possible. For example, 'The effects of age on users' perceptions of the usability of a speech-based mobile phone service' is better than 'An investigation into the effects of individual differences such as age when users are assessing the usability of a speech-based mobile phone service'.

Abstract

The abstract is also sometimes referred to as the summary. This may seem a bit strange having a summary right at the beginning of your report but there is a good reason for this. The idea of the abstract is to provide the reader with a summary of the main points of the report that you have painstakingly produced. This is very useful for people who are interested in your general topic and are conducting a literature review. If they can see a summary of the findings of your study, as well as information on your method, it could save them a lot of time. By looking at the abstract of projects from previous years, you will get some pointers on the design of your own final year project.

Introduction

In your introduction, you should introduce the subject area. For example, you may be interested in mobile phone designs for the elderly. In this case, you would start off by discussing HCI research that is related to the elderly. The next step would be to discuss some of the key theories and research work that are specific to mobile HCI and the elderly (this is still a relatively under-researched area, by the way). After this you should gradually narrow the focus to your particular study. The key here is to make a coherent argument that the reader (or any intelligent non-expert) can follow so that when you state the aims and objectives of your study they can understand where it fits in with the academic context you have just outlined.

Your aims and objectives should be clearly expressed. The aim of the project tells readers what your study is going to be about. For example, 'a user's perception of the usability of a speech-based versus keypad entry mobile phone service'. The objectives provide information on how you will achieve your project aim. For example, reviewing the relevant literature, developing a questionnaire to obtain information on users' perception of the usability of the two mobile phone services, and developing prototypes to use in your study.

Method

The next section of your report should contain information on the methods that you have chosen to use to investigate the aim of your study.

For example, if you are carrying out a mobile HCI experiment in the lab to investigate user preference for two different forms of input for a mobile phone service (e.g. speech versus keypad entry), you should provide details about the experimental design that you used (e.g. matched-pairs design or related measures design). You should also state what the dependent and independent variables will be in your experiment as well as how many participants will be used and what categories (*experimental conditions*) they will be placed into. In addition, you should mention what data collection techniques you are going to use (for example, time taken to complete a task, total number of errors made when completing a task, protocol analysis, etc.). For a re-cap on information about experimental design or data collection techniques for mobile HCI research projects, refer back to Chapters 3 and 4.

Something else that you may include in this section, if appropriate, is details of the prototyping method you used in your study. For example, you may have used a Wizard of Oz set-up to test users' perceptions of the two forms of interaction style (speech and keypad entry) for your study. Once again, to refresh your memory you can have a look at Chapter 5, which looks at prototyping techniques for mobile devices and applications.

Regardless of the methods that you choose to conduct your study, you must justify why you have chosen these methods.

Participants

You should provide relevant information on your participants. For example, you will want to tell the reader about how many participants took part in your study, how many males and how many females there were. You may want to say what age category (e.g. 18–30, 31–45, 46–55) participants fall into, describe what experience they have of using mobile phones services (e.g. novice users, in-frequent users, experienced users). In addition, you could provide information on the sampling method you used to get participants for your study (e.g. opportunistic, random or stratified). Information on sampling techniques can be found in Chapter 4.

Materials

In this section of your report, you should mention any apparatus or materials that you used in your study. For example, if you used a Likert-type questionnaire to assess users' perception of the system, you need to include examples of the statements used. You should also discuss how you designed the questionnaire (if relevant) and how you assessed its reliability and validity before you used it in your study. In addition, you should place a complete copy of the questionnaire in the appendix to your report.

If you used any technical equipment in your study, you should include information on that here too. For example, if you used a video camera to observe participants you should give details on the make and model that you used, as well as the set-up you employed to record data (e.g. were you discreetly filming people behind your newspaper in a café, or did you have the camera on a tri-pod next to the participants who were in your lab?).

In short, anything that you used to help you collect data should be described. Your reasons for choosing these materials and apparatus should be justified. This may seem extremely detailed to you. However, you should remember that someone may want to try and replicate your study or use parts of your method in their own study. Therefore, it's important that you provide as detailed an account of your investigation method as you can.

Procedure

In this section you have to describe as accurately as you can what happened in your study from start to finish. For example, imagine you wanted participants to attend your lab to assess the usability of the speech input and keypad entry versions of a new mobile phone service that allowed them to select music from a music catalogue. Here's how you might go about describing the procedure that was used in your study.

'On arriving at the lab to take part in the experiment, participants were given an oral/written explanation of the nature of the study by the experimenter. They were then asked if they had any questions relating to the study before being asked to sign the informed consent form. After a short break the participant was given a sheet of instructions describing how to use the automated catalogue and a list of music tracks they were required to order. At this point the participant either used a speech input or keypad input version of the automated music catalogue service. After completing the task, each participant completed a Likert attitude questionnaire. The session finished with a semi-structured interview where participants were *asked to comment on any aspect of the experience they had just gone through. Finally participants were asked if they had any other questions. After this they were paid and shown out of the lab by the experimenter.'*

Results

The key thing to remember here is that the presentation of results should answer the question or questions asked in your project aim or hypothesis. For example, in the study we have described so far in this section, we are interested in users' attitude to both versions of the service and also how they performed when using both services. Therefore, we could present our results on user performance as shown in Table 7.2.

The results displayed in Table 7.2 inform us that, apart from the youngest age group, participants in the study completed the tasks they were given more quickly when they used the speech input version of the automated music catalogue.

After presenting your main results from the performance data that you obtained from your study, you should present the main findings obtained from your attitude questionnaire and interviews with participants. For example, the interview was conducted to find out what participants thought about the automated mobile phone services that they used in the study. In order to analyse this data you may have conducted a thematic analysis (i.e. trying to look for themes emerging from the comments that people have made) of the transcripts that you collected. To display this data in your results section you could try something like Table 7.3.

In Table 7.3 the themes that emerged from the thematic analysis of the data are represented under the heading called '*Factor*'. For each factor there are direct quotes from participants to illustrate what this concept stands for. In this example they come under the heading of '*Comments to Support Factor*'.

In this section you may well combine your presentation of the data with details of any statistical analysis that you performed. For example, you may have decided to test whether there was any significant difference in the time it took participants to complete the tasks you set them using the speech input version of the automated mobile phone service in comparison to the touch tone entry version of the service. For information on how to present results obtained from data analysis see Coolican (2000) for a comprehensive review.

Table 7.2 Participants Average Task Completion Times in Seconds

Participant Age Group	Task 1 (Time in secs)		Task 2 (Time in secs)		Task 3 (Time in secs)	
	Speech	Key Pad	Speech	Key Pad	Speech	Key Pad
18–30	90	88	120	119	110	112
31–45	120	100	156	146	130	145
46–55	156	146	180	210	200	243

Table 7.3 Factors Affecting Users Perception of the Usability of the Service

Factor	Comments to Support Factor
Social acceptability	• I wouldn't like to use this type of service in public • I'd get embarrassed if I had to use this service sitting next to someone on the train • It's a mobile service, you're supposed to use it in public
Ease of use	• It was easy to learn how to use the service • Once, I had my practice session, it was easy to complete the tasks • The system was easy to use as it was consistent in its feedback all the time
Cognitive demand	• I felt I had to concentrate hard when using the service to complete my tasks • I sometimes felt lost in hyperspace when trying to get the information I wanted • Some of the menu options were too long, I forgot what option I wanted a few times
Previous experience	• I've had a mobile phone for a few years now so I'm used to using these types of services • I only got a mobile phone about six months ago, so I still get confused when I use a service I don't use very often
Speed of service	• The system was too slow, it seemed to take ages to respond to my requests • If you made a mistake it took along time to get back toy where you were before you made it • The prompts should have been shorter and a bit less formal

Discussion

To begin with, the discussion section should focus on talking about how your results relate to the original aims of your study. For example, were there differences in people's attitude scores towards the perceived usability of the speech-input version of the automated mobile phone service as opposed to the touch-tone version? Next, you should discuss how your results compared with other research that has been reported in this area. Remember you will be comparing your results with the research that you have mentioned in the Introduction section of your report.

What happens if you get 'unexpected' results? Well, you should discuss these too. Don't try and sweep them under the carpet. It could be that your results may lead to further research in a novel and interesting direction that you did not expect! It's crucial here to think about *why* you got these results. Could it have been down to the way you designed your experiment? For example, did you use the right data collection methods, did you choose the correct dependent and independent variables to study? Think about how your study differed from the findings reported by others.

It is important to *evaluate and reflect* upon your study in the discussion section. If there were any flaws in your design that you recognise now as having had an impact on the results that you obtained, you should mention these. If you did not get the results you were expecting it may not be down to design. For example, if your results don't actually show a significant difference in participants' preferences for speech over touch-tone for a new mobile phone service, but trend towards a preference for speech, say so. You can then discuss how you would explore this in a further study.

At this stage you can also discuss further research that could be undertaken to build upon the work that you have reported in your study. For example, could you conduct your study over a longer time? Another aspect that could be worth writing about is your personal reflections on the research work you have just carried out and the actual process of carrying out a research project.

Conclusions

Finally, you bring your report to an end by having a concluding paragraph in the discussion section or a separate conclusion section (depending on the report structure that you are working to). Here you should summarise the main findings of your study and briefly discuss how they relate to your original aims and how they fit in with previous research findings. You can also mention what the implications of your findings are for future work in this area.

This can be a surprisingly tricky section to write. Why? Well, it's important not to repeat what you have just said in the discussion section and it's also important not to repeat what you have written in the abstract or summary. Here's a tip for you. Even though the abstract is the first thing that people will read in your report, I would make it the last thing that you write. That way you'll be less likely to repeat yourself. Remember the aim of the abstract is to provide a summary of the whole study (e.g. aims, methods, results, conclusions) whereas the conclusion section provides a summary of your overall findings and where the work could go from here.

Appendices

Your appendices may contain the following types of information (depending on the nature of the study you have carried out):

- Copies of any test materials that you used in your study (e.g. usability questionnaire).
- Copies of instructions given to participants (e.g. tasks that they have to perform).
- Raw data (e.g. full transcripts of your interviews with participants, task completion timings).
- Screen shots of your prototype (you could also submit a full copy of the prototype system on CD).

You can refer your readers to the appendices in your report. Therefore, it is important that you give each appendix a unique identifier. For example, you could write something like this *'Please refer to Appendix A to see a full copy of the usability questionnaire that was used in this study'*, in the Materials section of your report.

Once again when it comes to producing appendices, it's important that you consult the guidelines for your report to make sure you don't omit something that the assessor is expecting. If in doubt, talk to your supervisor, I'm sure they'll be able to set you straight on that one!

Reference list

All work that you quote in your report should appear in your reference list at the end of your report. The people who assess your project will look carefully at your references and want to make sure that the references that you quote in your report are presented in your reference list.

They may deduct marks for reference lists that are incomplete and inaccurate. So be warned!

You should adopt a consistent approach to how you cite your references in your reference list. If in doubt, check with your supervisor to see if they want you to use a particular style. However, here is an example of a commonly used referencing approach, known as the Harvard style:

Books

Norman, D. A. (1988) *The Psychology of Everyday Things.* New York, Basic Books.

A reference that you use from an edited collection of work that appears in a book would be referenced as follows:

Murtagh, G. (2000) Seeing the 'Rules': Preliminary Observations of action, Interaction and Mobile Phone Use. In *Wireless World: Social and Interactional Aspects of the Mobile Age,* Brown, B., Green, N. & Harper, R. (Eds). London: Springer.

Journal article

Wei, R. and Leung, L. (1999) Blurring public and private behaviours in public space: policy challenges in the use and improper use of the cell phone. *Telematics and Informatics,* 16, 11–26.

Conference proceedings

Love, S. (2001) 'Space Invaders: Do Mobile Phone Conversations Invade Peoples' Personal Space?'. Proceedings of 18th International Human Factors in Telecommunications Symposium in Bergen, Norway, 5–7 November 2001, 125–131.

Internet reference

BT Cellnet (2001) Mobile Etiquette: Changing the way we use our mobiles. http://www.btcellnet.net/cgi-bin accessed 15/10/01.

In the case of an internet reference, as with all references, it is important that you make it as easy as possible for other people to find this article if they are interested in reading it.

Referencing reports with unknown authors

Sometimes you may quote a piece of work that comes from a group or organisation without any names given as to who wrote the report. In these cases you could reference this as follows:

The Disability Discrimination Act (1995). Chapter 50. Department for Education and Employment, UK.

OVERALL WRITING AND PRESENTATION STYLE

The chances are, you will be given guidelines of what your tutor expects in terms of your report format and structure. There may even be set institutional guidelines that you will be expected to follow. It's good to familiarise yourself with these requirements before you start to write your report. Things such as page numbers (on each page!) are useful, as are a table of contents, section headings and sub-headings. Also of importance is spelling, it's amazing the number of students who seem to forget that the all word processing packages have a spell checking facility! In terms of writing style, this is an individual thing. However, by the time you come to write your report you'll be familiar with (from all the reading you carried out as part of your literature review process) the 'academic' style of writing. If you can also access a previous dissertation (make sure that it is one that received a good grade) this will provide you with some useful pointers too.

It is essential that you write your report in a clear and informative way. You should work on the principle that an interested individual could pick up your report and walk away with a clear idea of what your study was about; why you chose to investigate it; what your findings were and what conclusions can be made from the result of this piece of work.

SUMMARY

The aim of this chapter was to provide you with a set of guidelines to help you plan and carry out a research project and it also gave you information on how to structure and write-up your project report.

You have to answer three questions before you start your project: (1) what will I study? (2) why should I study this topic?, and (3) how will I study this topic. The answers to these questions will come from topics you have covered in lectures; discussions with your tutor; talking over research ideas with friends and from carrying out a literature search.

The literature review will produce ideas about specific research questions that you can ask and what methods you can choose to help you investigate your research question. In relation to carrying out the project, it is important to plan and manage your project from the beginning and set yourself realistic milestones and time-scales for achieving these. In addition, it is also important to build in scope for contingency plans in case things don't go according to plan.

When it comes to writing up your project you must familiarise yourself with the departmental or institutional guidelines that you will be expected to follow. The project report was discussed in relation to its constituent parts, and information and advice was given in this chapter on how these sections could be presented in a way that is informative and interesting for the reader (especially the people who will be assessing your work!).

Hopefully, you will now realise that by planning and thinking about your project before you start, you can save a lot of time and effort in the long run. The same applies to the writing up and presentation of your report.

Self test

- Boolean operators
- Citation style
- Ethics
- Risk management

Exercises

1. Imagine you are about to undertake a final year project looking at the effects of age on users' perception of the usability of a new speech-based mobile phone service. You have six months to carry out this study. Produce a project plan (with project milestones included) that you think will allow you to carry out this project.

2. For the study mentioned above, create an informed consent form for participants to complete before they take part in your study.

3. Finally, what search statements would you use to help you find information on this research topic?

REFERENCES

Cairns, P. and Thimbleby, H. (2002) *The Diveristy and ethics of HCI.* www.uclic.ucl.ac.uk/harlod/ethics/tochiethics.pdf Accessed 12.01.05

Coolican, H. (2000) *Introduction to Research Methods and Statistics in Psychology,* 3rd edition. Hodder and Stoughton

Sharp, J., Peters, J. and Howard K. (2002) *The Management of a Student Research Project,* 3rd edition. Gower

SUGGESTED FURTHER READING

Howitt, D. and Cramer, D. (2000) *An Introduction to Statistics in Psychology: a complete guide for students.* Sage

Silverman, D. (2001) *Interpreting Qualitative Data: methods for analysing talk, text, and interaction,* 2nd edition. Sage

8

Data analysis

INTRODUCTION

This chapter focuses on how to analyse the data you have collected as part of your mobile HCI research study. All the statistical techniques covered in the chapter are explained by using specific mobile HCI examples. You may find it strange that you have to work through the formulas for each of the tests, given the ready availability of a number of commercial statistical software packages. However, I think that by going through the examples like this, you will have a better understanding of what tests you should use in relation to the research methods that you have chosen. At the end of this chapter is a list of references for further and more in-depth coverage of statistical techniques that you can use as part of your research methodology.

WHY DO YOU NEED STATISTICS?

Imagine you live in a world where everyone is the same; they are the same height, wear the same clothes, they all have the same taste in music and they all have the same needs and requirements when it comes to using mobile services and applications. If nothing varies between people then all that you need to know about people's attitude and performance when using mobile services and applications could be gathered from just one person. Just imagine how easy it would be to develop new applications if this was the case. Some people might say, rather harshly, that this is what happens already.

However, as you know, variability is an essential aspect of the world we live in and it has an impact in the area of human–computer interaction. So far, this book has highlighted aspects of variability (see Chapter 2 on user characteristics and Chapter 6 which deals with social usability) that could have a significant effect on mobile application uptake and design impact.

The aim of statistics in all of this is to help us to try and make sense of this variability. This variability is something you may have taken for granted as you developed your questionnaires, interview questions and chose your performance measures for use in our mobile HCI research. However, once you have that data you have to think about what you are going to do with it.

The first step you have to think about when you have your data is how you summarise the information that you have collected from the various sources, such as the ones discussed in Chapter 3. This sum-marising includes putting your data into a format that clearly explains the main features of your data, such as graphs, charts and tables. This aspect of statistics is referred to as *descriptive statistics*.

Describing data: numerically

Essentially, descriptive statistics are concerned with ways of presenting the data you have collected from your study. No-one wants to see your raw data – what they want is a summary of the main trends and differ-ences. Therefore, what you are presented with in most research reports (e.g. journal articles, conference proceedings) is what the researcher thinks are the main findings from their work. However, as you know, by summarising the main findings of your research you can distort the infor-mation that is actually presented (ask any politician). Therefore you, as an ethical mobile HCI researcher, should only be interested in presenting the clearest and least ambiguous picture of your data (even if it goes against your hypothesis). One important way of describing your data is known as the measure of central tendency. Let's have a look at this now.

Measures of central tendency

Measures of central tendency are known as the mean, median and mode. We will look at each of these in turn. The first thing we need though is

Table 8.1   People's Task Completion Time for
a Mobile Cinema Listing Service

Participant	Task Completion Time
1	35
2	32
3	40
4	10
5	35
6	27
7	25
8	35
9	33
10	34

an example of a data set to help us explain these measures. The example
in Table 8.1 shows a set of performance scores (based on time taken to
complete a task) obtained from a study that was carried out assessing
people's performance when using a mobile cinema listing service.

Mean
This is the technical term that is used when people are talking about the
average score for a data set. This is quite easy to calculate, all you have
to do is add up all the values that are in the table under the heading task
completion time and divide this by the total number of participants who
took part in the study. Therefore, using the example shown in Table 8.1
to calculate the mean task completion time for the people who took
part in our study, the calculation is as follows:

$$\frac{35 + 32 + 40 + 10 + 35 + 27 + 25 + 35 + 33 + 34}{10}$$

According to my calculations the mean task completion time for participants in the example study highlighted above is 30.6.

   To calculate the mean we have used a *formula*. A formula is just a set
of instructions that you should follow in order to find out, in this

instance, what the mean is for the data set that you are interested in analysing. The formula used is as follows:

$$\overline{X} = \frac{\Sigma x}{N}$$

Using formulas is a bit like following recipes – if you do it correctly you'll get the desired result. We will be using a number of different formulas in this chapter.

In the above example, the expressions that make up the formula for calculating the mean can be described as follows: $\overline{X}$ = this is the statistical term that is used to describe the arithmetic mean of a sample population (in the example above, it is 30.6); Σx = this expression tells you that you should add up all the scores (in the example we are using there are 10 scores to be added up). In case you are wondering, Σ is the Greek letter S (pronounced 'sigma') and when you see this used in a formula it means that you should add up 'each that follows'. In our example it is the 10 attitude scores; N = the next part of the formula tells you that you should divide the total of these scores by the number (N) of scores contained in the sample. In this case N = 10.

Median
The median is the central value of a data set (i.e. 50 per cent of the numbers in the data set are above the median number and 50 per cent of the numbers in the data set are below it). In order to calculate the median you have to arrange the values in the data set in rising numerical order. Therefore, using the example data set above, the data would be arranged as shown in Table 8.2.

The formula for calculating the median position (or location as it's also sometimes referred to) is as follows:

$$\frac{N+1}{2}$$

To work out the position of the median you would have to calculate the following statistic:

$$\frac{10+1}{2}$$

The answer to this is 5.5. Therefore, the median will be midway between the values positioned 5 and 6 in our data set. In this case value 5 = 33

Table 8.2   Task Completion
Times in Ascending Order

Task Completion Times in Ascending Order
10
25
27
32
33
34
35
35
35
40

and value 6 = 34. Therefore, the median value for this data set would be an attitude score of 33.5.

One of the advantages that the median has over the mean as a measure of central tendency is that it is unaffected by extreme scores in one direction. For example, if someone had an extremely positive score in a data set whilst the rest of the data was more neutral, calculating the mean could give a false impression of the extent to which people actually liked using a particular service. However, unlike the mean, it does not use the exact values for each item when making its calculation. Another potential disadvantage is that if your data set is small, it can be quite unrepresentative too. For example, if you only had five participants in your study and their attitude scores are as follow: 8, 10, 19, 38, 40, the median would be 19. How accurate a reflection of the average attitude towards the service would this be? This can also be a drawback of using the men as a measure of central tendency.

Mode
The mode is actually the easiest of the three measures of central tendency to calculate. All you have to do is find the value that occurs most in your data set. That is, you have to calculate the frequency (f) of all scores and see which ones has the highest frequency. For the example

Table 8.3   Calculating the Modal Score

Task Completion Times	Frequency (f) of Score
10	1
25	1
27	1
32	1
33	1
34	1
35	3
40	1

that we have been using to explain measures of central tendency, we can see from Table 8.3 that the modal value for this data set is 35.

You can also have data sets where there is no single mode as there may be some scores that share the highest frequency. When you have a distribution of scores where two share the highest frequency this is known as a *bimodal distribution*. If you have several scores sharing the highest frequency this is known a *multimodal distribution*.

Describing data: tables and diagrams

Another way of describing the main trends and outcomes of the data you have collected from your mobile HCI research is to summarise the main findings in tables and diagrams. As we have seen in relation to the discussion on measures of central tendency, it is not very helpful for a reader to have to wade through all the raw data that you collected in order to find out the main findings of your study. Therefore, by using tables and graphs you have the opportunity to structure your data in a way that allows the reader to quickly see the main outcomes of your study. One key rule to remember is that if your tables and diagrams are unclear or difficult to understand, they are useless. Here are some examples of how to present your data in a clear and informative way.

The first example, shown in Table 8.4, is one that you will remember from earlier in the chapter (hopefully). The second example, shown in Figure 8.1, indicates how you can use a bar chart to represent different groups of participants' (based on age groups) attitudes towards two

Table 8.4 Participants Task Completion
Times for a Mobile Cinema Listing Service

Participant	Task Completion Times
1	35
2	32
3	40
4	10
5	35
6	27
7	25
8	35
9	33
10	34

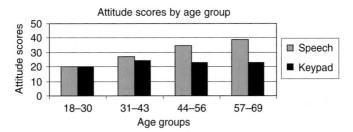

Figure 8.1 Attitude towards the speech and keypad version of the service based
on age group

versions of a mobile phone service: a speech-based service and a keypad version of the service.

There are two key things to remember when you are producing your
tables and diagrams:

1. Make sure that your table or diagram has a concise heading that
   accurately describes the information contained within it.
2. Label everything in your table or diagram as clearly as possible. For
   example, this includes giving a name to both axes if you are using
   a graph to illustrate your data and clearly labelling the different
   categories in your histogram or bar chart.

Types of measurement

In all good statistics books you will find information on *scales of measurement*. These essentially fall into two main categories: numerical measurement and categorical measurement. It is important that you understand what these scale are for the differences between them. If you don't, you may end up trying to apply an incorrect statistical method to a set of data, and drawing the wrong conclusions from the results of your analysis.

Numerical measurement

As the name suggests, numerical scales of measurement provide you with some form of numerical value or score. This includes many of the measures used to collect data in mobile HCI research. For example, it could be the amount of time it takes each participant in your study to complete a task using a new mobile cinema listing service. This form of numerical measurement would be classed as an *interval scale* of measurement as time (as you know) is made up of equal units of measurement. In this case the distance between values obtained on the scale is important. For example, you know that someone taking 36 seconds to complete a task using the new cinema listing service took almost three times as long as someone who took 12 seconds to complete the same task. Alternatively, you may ask participants to rank in order of importance (from a given list) the key features that a new mobile cinema listing service should have. This form of measurement scale would be classed an *ordinal scale*, as you are ordering the features on a given dimension (e.g. order of importance). However, in this instance, you do not have any information about what the distance between these positions actually means.

Another form of numerical measurement comes in the form of 'invented scales'. For example, you may create a Likert attitude questionnaire (this process is described in Chapter 3) to assess participants' attitude towards the usability of a new mobile phone-based cinema listing service.

Category measurement

This type of measurement (also known as the *nominal scale*) requires you to allocate a particular unit of data to a specific category. For example, imagine you had created an observation sheet (Chapter 3 on research methods explains how to go about this) to assess how people reacted when they were on a crowded train and the person next to them started using their mobile phone. You may have categories such as 'looked out of window', 'looked angrily at the person using their phone'. This form of measurement is known as a nominal measurement as the categories are given names like the ones we've described above. One thing to bear in mind in relation to this form of measurement is that there are no numbers involved in the categorisation. All you are doing is adding up the frequencies for the number of times each of the behaviours you described in your observational headings occurred. Therefore, the numbers are not related to one single measurement but the total of the frequencies (i.e. number of occurrences) of that particular category.

Parametric and non-parametric statistics

At some point in your research career you will come across the terms *parametric test* and *non-parametric test* when reading up on data analysis techniques. Therefore, it is important, even in this brief introduction to statistics for mobile HCI research, that you understand the difference between these two sets of tests.

Parametric tests are powerful tests based on the assumption that the data you have collected from your study is *normally distributed* according to some specific underlying distribution. For example, imagine you carried out a study investigating people's performance (based on timings for completing a specific task) when using a mobile phone cinema listing service. After you have collected the data, you could put timings data into a histogram to view what the distribution of scores is like. If it is normally distributed, it will look like the histogram shown in Figure 8.2.

This shape, known as the bell-curve, suggests that the data you have collected is distributed normally across your sample population. If this is the case, you can use parametric tests to detect if there is a significant

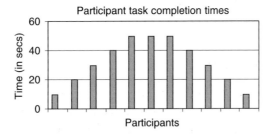

Figure 8.2   Example of normal distribution based on task completion times

difference associated with the independent variable (if you can't remember what an independent variable is, have a quick look back at Chapter 3) used in your study. For example, you could assess whether there is any difference between males and females in your study in relation to the length of time it took them to complete their tasks.

However, in some cases, when you put your data into a histogram you will notice that it is not exactly bell-shaped. Luckily, parametric tests are fairly robust and can accommodate for distributions that are not exactly normal. However, if your data looks really skewed (i.e. there is a peak at one end of the histogram or the other) it may be worth consulting a statistical textbook such as Coolican (2000) to find ways of carrying out tests on the data to assess if you can reliably use parametric statistics. As well as assuming a normal distribution of your data, parametric tests also assume that the data you have collected comes from an interval scale (e.g. a performance measure such as task completion time, or the number of errors made when completing a task).

Non-parametric tests, on the other hand, do not rely on any underlying assumptions about the probability distribution of the sampled population. Therefore, some people use non-parametric tests when they have looked at the distribution of their data and have come to the conclusion that they cannot justify the use of parametric tests because it is skewed. In addition, non-parametric tests are used when the data is collected in the form of rankings (e.g. ordinal scales) or frequency counts (e.g. categorical scales). For example, imagine you were interested in designing a new PDA application and had a list of features that you think the application should have. However, being a good mobile HCI designer, you want to find out what potential users rate are the most important features to have. Therefore, you get various groups of representative users (e.g. older users, younger users) into your lab and ask them to rate in order of importance the features they believe the PDA application should have. In order to test for differences in terms of preference between the users groups, you would carry out the appropriate non-parametric tests based on the rankings you obtained from the participants in your study. Some statisticians (e.g. Coolican, 2000), also suggest that data collected from 'invented scales' (e.g. Likert usability questionnaires) should be analysed using non-parametric tests, as these types of measurement scales do not produce *true* interval data.

Therefore, as you may have collected data using different types of measurement scales as part of your mobile HCI research, I have included examples of both parametric and non-parametric tests in this chapter.

TESTING FOR DIFFERENCES

The first sets of test we will look at are known as *tests of difference*. In these tests you want to know if there is any significant difference between people's score on the independent variable (if you can't remember what the independent variable is, have a quick look back at Chapter 3). The first two tests to be discussed in this section are the related *t*-test and the unrelated *t*-test. These are parametric tests. The second two tests that are discussed, the Mann-Whitney U and the Wilcoxon, are non-parametric tests.

Related *t*-test

This test is commonly used when you want to compare the differences between two groups of numbers that have come from a repeated measures design or matched-pairs design. For example, imagine you have carried out a study comparing people's performance when using two versions of a mobile cinema listing service: speech input and keypad input. In order to assess user performance you timed how long it took each participant to complete a specific task (e.g. finding the cinema opening times). In the example we are using here, our data has come from a repeated measures design as our participants used both versions of the mobile phone service. If you are unsure about these terms go back to Chapter 3 and re-fresh your memory. It may actually be worth your while to book mark that chapter while you go through this chapter, just in case.

Let's go through how to carry out this test in Technical Tip 1.

Technical Tip 1

Related *t*-test

You have 10 participants who took part in your study to assess people's performance when using a speech-based cinema listing and booking service in comparison to a keypad version of the same service. In order to collect data on this, you asked participants to complete a specific task (e.g. find out the cinema opening times) and timed them on how long it took to complete the task. You have adopted a repeated measures design and counter-balanced your order of use to control for order effects (remember we discussed the importance of counter-balancing your design in Chapter 3).

Table 8.5   Participant Task Completion Times in mins for Speech and Keypad Versions of the Service

Participant Number	Task Completion Times (Speech)	Task Completion Times (Keypad)
1	5.6	4.3
2	6.7	5.6
3	4.8	6.6
4	3.7	6.1
5	6.8	4.3
6	7	5.1
7	5.5	5.2
8	6.7	4.3
9	6.7	4.9
10	5.9	4.8

After you have collected the data, you put it into a spread sheet. At this stage your data file should look something like that shown in Table 8.5.

Now that you have this data, you are ready to carry out a related *t*-test. The formula for this is as follows:

$$t = \frac{\Sigma d}{\sqrt{\left(\dfrac{N \, \Sigma d^2 - [\Sigma d]^2}{N - 1} \right)}}$$

I know that this formula may be off-putting but let's work out what all the elements are in this expression and then we can substitute letters for actual data to allow use to carry this out. Here is a step-by-step guide to calculating the components for the mathematical expression:

1. The first thing you have to do is to calculate the difference in scores between the speech and keypad conditions and then add these (also sometimes referred to as sum) up – Σd
2. The next step is to square these differences – $(\Sigma d)^2$
3. After this, square the differences between the two sets of scores first and then add them up – Σd^2
4. It's important not to get step 2 and step 3 mixed up, so be careful!

5. Finally calculate the number of pairs of scores in your data set – *N*
   Once you have carried out these calculations all you have to do is to substitute actual numbers in place of the mathematical expressions and you are ready to calculate your related *t*-test. It is also probably a good idea to have a calculator handy when you get to this point too.

6. According to my calculations, your equation should be looking something like this:

$$t = \frac{8.2}{\sqrt{\left(\frac{(10 \times 32.06) - 67.24}{10 - 1}\right)}}$$

7. Now calculate the *t* statistic. My *t* value comes out as *t* = 1.55, what about you?

8. The next step is to calculate the degrees of freedom. This is calculated as follows: *df* = *N* − 1. In our case this is 10 − 1. Therefore the *df* = 9.

9. Now you are ready to see if your results are statistically significant. In order to do this, consult Table A1 in Appendix A. As we did not make any predictions about which service would be perceived more favourably than the other, we are interested in the critical *t* values for a two-tailed test. If we had made a prediction that it would be quicker to find the cinema opening times quicker using one service than the other service, we would be looking at columns related to one-tailed values.

10. Look for the column where it says *df* = 9. If your value of *t* is larger than the value listed in that column we can say that you found a significant difference in user performance between the two versions of the mobile phone service at the 5 per cent level ($p < 0.05$). If it is lower, we do not find a significant difference in performance scores between the two versions of the cinema listing and booking service. As you can see from Table A1, in relation to our example, our reported value (1.55) is lower than the figure listed, therefore this indicates that we did not find a significant difference between the two conditions.

11. The final thing to mention here is how to report this finding in your written report. Conventionally you would report this finding as follows: *t* = 1.55, *df* = 9, two-tailed ns (where ns stands for not significant).

Unrelated *t*-test

Imagine that you were carrying out a study looking at potential gender differences when people are using information services via an internet-enabled PDA. One way you might go about this is to get a group of males and females to use this device to find out information on local train services. In order to look for gender differences, you may time how long it takes both sets of participants to find information on the train times you asked them to look for. Once you have this data, you naturally want to check to see if there is a significant statistical difference in the amount of time it takes males and females to find this information. The test you would use to help you here is the unrelated *t*-test (also known as the independent *t*-test).

This test is commonly used when you want to compare the differences between two sets of data that have come from an unrelated design. In the example we are using here, our data has come from an unrelated design as data has been collected from two different groups of participants (i.e. females and males). Let's look at how to carry out this test in Technical Tip 2.

Technical Tip 2

Calculating an unrelated *t*-test

You have 20 participants who took part in your study to compare search times between males and females when they are using a PDA service to find out train departure times. You would have collected this type of data by timing how long it takes each participant to find the train departure times that you asked them to. The raw data might look something like Table 8.6.

Now that you have this data, you are ready to carry out an unrelated *t*-test. The formula for this is as follows:

$$t = \frac{\bar{x}_A - \bar{x}_B}{\sqrt{\frac{\left[\left(\Sigma x_A^2 - \frac{(\Sigma x_A)^2}{N_A}\right) + \left(\Sigma x_B^2 - \frac{(\Sigma x_B)^2}{N_B}\right)\right]}{(N_A + N_B - 2)}\left[\frac{N_A + N_B}{(N_A)(N_B)}\right]}}$$

Now if you found the formula off-putting for the related *t*-test, I don't really know what you will think of this one. However, persevere, this one can be easily explained too.

Table 8.6   Gender Search Times

Group A: Female Search Times (In Seconds)	Group B: Male Search Times (In Seconds)
176	190
256	245
278	260
187	185
260	245
234	189
190	230
184	187
293	190
193	180

Step-by-step guide to calculating the components for the mathematical expression:

1. The first thing to do is to calculate the number of people in group A – N_A
2. Next calculate the number of people in group B – N_B
3. Next add up all the scores in group A – Σx_A
4. Next add up all the scores in group B – Σx_B
5. Square each score in group A and then add all these up – Σx_A^2
6. Square each score in group B and then add all these up – Σx_B^2
7. Calculate the mean of the scores in group A – $\bar{x}_A$
8. Calculate the mean of the scores in group B – $\bar{x}_B$
9. According to my calculations, your equation should be looking something like this:

$$t = \cfrac{225.1 - 210.1}{\sqrt{\cfrac{\left[\left[524,175 - \cfrac{(2251)^2}{10}\right] + \left[450,065 - \cfrac{(2101)^2}{10}\right]\right]}{(10 + 10 - 2)}\left[\cfrac{10 + 10}{(10)(10)}\right]}}$$

10. Now calculate the *t* statistic. My *t* value comes out as 0.89, what about you?

11. The next step is to calculate the degrees of freedom. This is calculated as follows:

$df = N_A + N_B - 2$. In our case this is $20 - 2$. Therefore, the $df = 18$.

12. Now you are ready to see if your results are statistically significant. In order to this, consult Table A1 in Appendix A. As we did not make any predictions about which group would find the information on train times quicker than the other, we are interested in the critical t values for a two-tailed test. If we had made a prediction that females would find the train departure information quicker than males, we would be looking at columns related to one-tailed values.

13. Once you have your tails sorted out, look for the column where it says $df = 18$. If your value of t is larger than the figure listed in that column we can say that you have found a significant difference in search times between females and males at the 5 per cent level ($p < 0.05$). If it is lower, we did not find a significant difference in search times between males and females in your study. The final thing to mention here is how to report this finding in your written report. Conventionally you would report this finding as follows: $t = 0.89$, $df = 18$, two-tailed ns (where ns stands for not significant). This could be written out more formally as the mean time taken for females to find train departure information (M = 225.1 secs) using the PDA application is not significantly quicker than the average time taken by male users (M = 210.1 secs), $t = 0.89$, $df = 18$, two-tailed ns.

Wilcoxon signed-ranks test

This test should be used if you have a two condition related design, using the same participants (or matched participants) to participate in both conditions. The aim of this test is to compare participants' performance in the two conditions to find out whether or not there is any difference between the scores obtained. This test is the non-parametric equivalent of the related t-test. The example we will use here will be data from a group of participants who used two different methods of interaction to carry out a web search using a PDA device. The first condition required participants to use a stylus to interact with the application and the second condition required them to use keypad entry. After using each version of the application participants were asked to rate the usability of the device using a Likert-type questionnaire. Let's look at Technical Tip 3 to work through how to calculate this statistic.

Calculating a Wilcoxon singed-ranks test

The data obtained from this study comes from the attitude score obtained from each participant on the Likert usability scale described above. The scale was based on a 7-point scale. The higher the overall usability score, the more positively the participant rated the PDA application. Table 8.7 provides information on what the initial data table may look like:

1. The first step in working out this formula is to calculate the difference between each pair of scores, assigning plus or minus signs where appropriate.
2. The next step is to rank the differences between the scores obtained for the two conditions (ignoring the plus or minus signs this time).
3. After that, rank the plus difference and rank the minus differences.
4. Your data table should now look something like Table 8.8.
5. The next step is to take the smaller of the totals obtained for the plus and minus rank differences. This gives us the value of a statistic called W (remember this is called the Wilcoxon test) and this will be used to look up the appropriate table for statistical significance.
6. The next step is to calculate the number of pairs of participants that do not have tied scores. From the example above we can see that there are no tied pairs of scores, therefore in this case $N = 10$. However, if

Table 8.7 Participant Attitude Scores for Stylus Input and Keypad Entry

Participant	Stylus Input Attitude Score	Keypad Entry Attitude Score
1	25	38
2	24	39
3	32	37
4	29	36
5	38	34
6	31	30
7	27	31
8	39	40
9	21	35
10	22	33

Table 8.8   Initial Data Table for Calculating a Wilcoxon Signed-ranks Test

Participant	Stylus	Keypad	Difference (d)	Rank of d	Rank of +	Rank of −
1	25	38	−13	8 (−)		6
2	24	39	−15	10 (−)		8
3	32	37	−5	5 (−)		3
4	29	36	−7	6 (−)		4
5	38	34	4	3.5 (+)	2	
6	31	30	1	1.5 (+)	1	
7	27	31	−4	3.5 (−)		2
8	39	40	−1	1.5 (−)		1
9	21	35	−14	9 (−)		7
10	22	33	−11	7 (−)		5
Total					3	39

> you do get any tied pairs of scores, subtract the number of tied scores from the total number of paired scores to obtain your value of N.
>
> 7. The next step is to look up Table A2 in Appendix A to find out if the result obtained from this data is statistically significant. As we did not make a prediction about which version of the PDA application that participants would prefer, we are only interested in significance levels for two-tailed tests.
> 8. When assessing the significance (or not) of your obtained value of W, remember that it is classed as being significant if it is equal to, or less than the stated value in the table. From looking at Table A2, it shows that the result for this example is significant ($p < 0.02$).
> 9. How can this be interpreted? Well the result suggests that people have a more positive attitude towards the keypad entry version of the PDA application than they have for the stylus input version.
> 10. If you were writing this result up formally you would write something like the following: Participants had a significantly more positive attitude towards the keypad entry version of the PDA application than the stylus input version, $W = 3, p < 0.02$).

Mann-Whitney U-test

This test should be used if you have a two condition unrelated design, using the different participants to participate in both conditions. This is the non-parametric equivalent of the unrelated *t*-test. The example we will use here will be similar to the example we used for the Wilcoxon test outlined above. However, this time, the data will come from two different groups of participants who used the two different versions of the PDA device. The first condition required participants to use a stylus to interact with the application and the second condition required the second group of participants to use keypad entry. After using each version of the application participants were asked to rate the usability of the device using a Likert-type questionnaire. Let's look at Technical Tip 4 to work through how to calculate this statistic.

Technical Tip 4

Calculating a Mann-Whitney U-test

The data obtained from this exercise came in the form of total scores for each participant on the usability scale. The scale was based on a 7-point scale. Once again, the higher the overall usability score, the more positively the participant rated the PDA application. The initial data table may look like Table 8.9.

1. The formula for working out the Mann-Whitney U statistic is as follows:

$$U = N_1 N_2 + \frac{N_x(N_x + 1)}{2} - T_x$$

Table 8.9 Participant Attitude Scores

Stylus Input Attitude Score	Keypad Entry Attitude Score
24	38
24	39
32	37
29	36
38	34
31	30
27	31
31	40
21	35
31	33

2. The expressions used in the formula can be defined as follows:
   N_1 = the total number of participants in group 1
   N_2 = the total number of participants in group 2
   N_x = total number of participants in the group with the largest rank total
   T_x = the largest rank total score
3. In order to get data to put in these expressions, you will have to carry out some calculations on your original data table. When it comes to ranking the scores, you should rank the scores for both groups as *a single series of ranks*. Once you have done this, your data should look like Table 8.10.
4. Your formula should now look something like this:

$$U = 10 \times 10 + \frac{10 \times 11}{2} - 143$$

5. According to my calculations $U = 512$.
6. The next step is to look up Table A3 in Appendix A to find out if the result obtained from this data is statistically significant. As we did not make a prediction about which version of the PDA application participants would prefer, we are only interested in significance levels for two-tailed tests.

Table 8.10   Data Table for Carrying out Mann-Whitney U Calculation

Stylus Input Attitude Score (group 1)	Rank (1)	Keypad Entry Attitude score (group 2)	Rank (2)
24	2.5	38	17.5
24	2.5	39	19
32	10.5	37	16
29	5	36	15
38	17.5	34	13
31	8	30	6
27	4	32	10.5
31	8	40	20
21	1	35	14
31	8	33	12
Total 288	68	353	143

7. When assessing the significance (or not) of your obtained value of U, remember that is classed as being significant if it is equal to, or less than the critical value in the table. From looking at Table A3, it shows that the result for this example is not significant.

8. If you were writing this result up formally you would write something like: Participants did not have a significantly more positive attitude towards the keypad entry version of the PDA application than the stylus input version ($U = 512$, ns).

CORRELATIONS

The idea behind a correlation is that you are looking for a relationship between two sets of numbers. To explain what I mean, have a look the following statements:

1. The warmer it gets, the more sales of sun protection products increase.
2. The more experience you have of using a mobile phone service, the quicker you become when using it.

The first statement is an example of what is known as a *positive correlation*. For example, as one variable increases, so does the other variable. Hopefully you can see that as it gets warmer the sales of sun protection products should increase too. The second statement is an example of what is known as a *negative correlation* whereby as one variable increases, the other variable decreases. In the second example, we would expect that as your experience of using a particular mobile phone service (such as an automated cinema listing service) increases, the rate at which you can use the service to find the particular type of information you are interested in decreases.

However, what about this statement: people who obtain A grades on psychology courses are also good at golf. This should be seen as an example of no correlation between two variables (e.g. psychology aptitude does not relate to people's golf skills).

You can calculate the strength of the relationship between two variables as long as you can pair the values. The actual correlation statistic that you calculate can range from -1 to 0, and from 0 to $+1$. A correlation that has a value between -1 and 0, indicates a negative relationship (i.e. the more experience that people have using a mobile phone service, the quicker you become when using it). Perhaps not surprisingly, a correlation statistic that has a value between 0 and +1 indicates a positive relationship between the two sets of values (i.e. the warmer it gets, the more the sales of sun cream increase).

The two correlation measures that we discuss in this section are: Pearson's Product Moment-Moment Correlation, which is a parametric test and Spearman's Rho, which is a non-parametric test.

Pearson's Product–Moment Correlation

The example we will use to explain this parametric statistical test is as follows. Is there a relationship between task performance and age when using a speech-based mobile phone train timetable information service? Using this example you can see that this test would be used when you have a related measures design for your study. Let's go through how to calculate this test in Technical Tip 5.

Technical Tip 5

Calculating a Pearson Product-Moment Correlation

You have 10 Participants in the age range 18 to 65, and they have all completed a specific task (e.g. find the time of the last train to Glasgow Central) to assess their performance when using a new speech-based mobile phone train timetable information service. The performance measure was based on the number of errors that participants made when completing this task. Your raw data looks something like that presented in Table 8.11.

1. Here is the formula that we will use to test if there is a relationship between age and performance when using the speech-based train timetable information service. Once again, it may look a bit complicated. However, we'll go through it in the same way we approached the t-tests and hopefully it won't seem too bad.

$$r = \frac{N \, \Sigma(XY) - \Sigma X \, \Sigma Y}{\sqrt{\left[N \, \Sigma X^2 - \left(\Sigma X\right)^2\right]\left[N \, \Sigma Y^2 - \left(\Sigma Y\right)^2\right]}}$$

2. The first thing to do is to set up columns that will allow you to calculate the parts of the formula that you need. In this case X represents the age of participants and Y represents the error scores of participants. Your initial table should look something like Table 8.12.

Table 8.11 Participants' Error Scores

Participant	Age	Attitude Score
1	18	7
2	20	6
3	21	6
4	35	8
5	39	5
6	45	3
7	65	2
8	60	2
9	56	1
10	52	3

Table 8.12 Data Table for a Spearman Product Moment Calculation

XY	X^2	Y^2
126	324	49
120	400	36
126	441	36
280	1225	64
195	1521	25
135	2025	9
110	4225	4
120	3600	4
56	3136	1
156	2704	9

3. After you have done this, use these scores to calculate the other parts of the formula that you need.

$$\Sigma x = 411$$

$$\Sigma y = 43$$

$$\Sigma xy = 1424$$

$$\Sigma x^2 = 19601$$

$$\Sigma y^2 = 237$$

4. After this, your formula should be looking something like this:

$$r = \frac{14240 - 17673}{\sqrt{[196070 - 168921][2370 - 1849]}}$$

5. After working out this formula, Pearson's $r = -0.91$, so this suggests that there is a strong negative correlation between age and performance when using a speech-based mobile phone train timetable information service.

6. The next step is to compare this value against those in Table A4 in Appendix A of this book to assess if your result is significant or not. The critical value for r at $p < 0.05$ is 0.56. The value of our r is above that and it is also higher than for the value given for r at $p < 0.01$ (0.79). Therefore, we can now confidently say you have a significant negative correlation between age and performance when using a speech-based mobile phone train timetable information service.

7. The way you should report this finding when you are writing about it in your report is as follows. A statistically significant correlation was found between age and performance when using a speech-based mobile phone train timetable information service ($r = -0.91$, $p < 0.01$). How can this be interpreted? Well, if you go back and look at the raw data presented in Table 8.11, you can see that as age increases, performance when using the speech-based mobile phone train timetable information service decreases, thus giving you a negative correlation.

Now that we've had a look at Pearson's Product-Moment Correlation, let's turn our attention to Spearman's Rho.

Spearman's Rho

The example I will use to explain this non-parametric statistical test is that you are conducting a study investigating the relationship between age and people's attitude to using a speech-based location aware device. Using this example you can see that this test would be used when you have a related measures design for your study. Let's go through how to calculate this test in Technical Tip 6. One point to note is that Spearman's Rho should only really be used when you do not have many tied ranks in your data set, or a small number of them.

Calculating a Spearman's Rho Correlation

There are 10 participants in this study, aged between 18 and 65, and they have all completed a Likert attitude questionnaire that assesses their use of mobile phones in public places. The maximum score an individual partic- ipant can obtain is 40 (which indicates a very positive attitude) and the lowest score is zero (indicating a very negative attitude). Your raw data may look something like Table 8.13.

1. Here is the formula that we will use to test if there is a relationship between age and attitude towards using mobile phones in public places.

$$r_S = 1 - \frac{6 \, \Sigma d^2}{N(N^2 - 1)}$$

Table 8.13 Spearman's Rho Data Table

Participant	Age	Attitude Score
1	18	7
2	20	6
3	21	6
4	35	8
5	35	5
6	45	3
7	65	2
8	60	2
9	60	1
10	52	3

Once again, it may look a bit complicated. However, we'll go through it in the same way we approached the other tests and hopefully it won't seem too bad.

2. The first thing to do is to set up your columns that will allow you to calculate the parts of the formula that you need. In this case, the age of participants is classed as group A, and the attitude scores obtained from participants is group B. The first thing you have to do is rank the scores from the lowest score to the highest score. Therefore your initial table should look something like Table 8.14.

Table 8.14 Data Table for Calculating Spearman's Rho Correlation

Age	Rank A	Attitude Score	Rank B	d	d^2
18	1	7	9	−8	64
20	2	6	7.5	−5.5	30.25
21	3	6	7.5	−4.5	20.25
35	4.5	8	10	−5.5	30.25
35	4.5	5	6	−1.5	2.25
45	6	3	4.5	1.5	2.25
65	10	2	2.5	7.5	56.25
60	8.5	2	2.5	6	36
60	8.5	1	1	7.5	56.25
52	7	3	4.5	2.5	6.25

3. After you have done this, use these scores to calculate the other parts of the formula that you need.
4. After this, your formula should be looking something like this:

$$r_S = 1 - \frac{6 - 304}{10(100 - 1)}$$

5. Spearman's rho (p) equals −0.84, so this suggests, once again, that there is a significant relationship between age and attitude towards using a mobile phone in public locations.
6. The next step is to compare this value against those in Table A5 in Appendix A to assess whether your result is significant or not. The critical value for r at $p < 0.05$ is 0.564. As our observed value is 0.84, we can conclude that this is a significant finding.

7. The way you should report this finding when you are writing about it in your report is as follows. The results reveal a statistically significant correlation between age and attitude towards mobile phone use in public places ($r = 0.15$, $p < 0.01$).

One thing that you should be aware of when you are trying to interpret your correlation results is that correlation does not imply causation. What does this mean? I hear you ask. It means that you can't assume that one variable has a causal effect on the other one. For example, although you might find there is a relationship between age and attitude towards mobile phone use in public places, this could be related to the fact that older people may not have thought they need to use the types of services that people normally use mobile phones in public for.

ANALYSING CATEGORICAL DATA

This type of analysis requires you to allocate your participants to specific category scales (i.e. nominal data scales) rather than acquiring data from them in ways similar to what we've already discussed in this chapter (e.g. attitude scores or performance measures such as time taken to complete a task). For example, this type of data can be obtained from information recorded by the researcher in an observational coding form (observational coding forms were one of the research approaches discussed in Chapter 3). A test that can be used to assess for statistical significance for data collected in this way is called the CHI-square Test (also written as χ^2). This will be the first test discussed in this section of the chapter.

Alternatively, you can collect qualitative information from participants in the form of open-ended questions (e.g. what did you like about the mobile tourist information guide?), and attempt to put the qualitative information obtained from these questions into categories in order to quantify the data. This approach is known as *content analysis* and it the second technique to be discussed in this section of the chapter.

CHI-square test

The CHI-square test is used when you have collected data in the form of frequencies and it is traditionally used in an unrelated design. As ever, the best way to explain this test is to work through an example together and this is shown in Technical Tip 7.

Calculating a CHI-square test

The data you have collected for this study comes from the observations made by a researcher over a period of two days in a busy café. The researcher was interested in assessing if there were any gender differences in relation to whether or not an individual would answer their mobile phone if they were in the company of other people. In order to carry out this study, the researcher followed the instructions given in Chapter 3 to create an observational coding form. At the end of the observation period, the researcher had collected the following data displayed here in Table 8.15.

1. The first thing that you have to do is to give the observed frequencies a letter for each cell (this should explain any confusion you may have had about the letters a-d appearing in Table 8.15).
2. The next step is to calculate the expected frequencies for each cell using this formula:

$$E = \frac{RC}{T}$$

E = expected frequency for a particular cell (a,b,c or d)
R = total of row cells (a + b) or (c + d)
C = total of column cells (a + c) or (b + d)
T = total of all cells (a + b + c + d)

So, the Expected frequency for the four cells in this example should be as follows:

$$E_a = \frac{129 \times 131}{257} = 65.8$$

Table 8.15   Frequency Data Obtained from Observational Coding Form

	Female	Male	Total
Had conversation	40 (a)	89 (b)	129
Did not have conversation	91 (c)	37 (d)	128
Total	131	126	257

$$E_b = \frac{129 \times 126}{257} = 63.2$$

$$E_c = \frac{128 \times 131}{257} = 65.2$$

$$E_d = \frac{128 \times 126}{257} = 62.8$$

The next step is to calculate the value of the χ^2 by using the following formula:

$$\chi^2 = \Sigma \frac{(O - E)^2}{E}$$

3. Remember that you have to calculate the following part of the formula for each of the four cells first:

$$\frac{(O - E)^2}{E}$$

To make this step easier to calculate, arrange your data similar to Table 8.16.

4. According to my calculations the final calculation should look something like:

$$\chi^2 = 10.1 + 10.5 + 10.2 + 10.5 = 43.3$$

Table 8.16 Data Table for Calculating a CHI-Square Test

Cell Number	Observed Frequency (O)	Expected Frequency (E)	$(O - E)$	$(O - E)^2$	$(O - E)^2/E$
A	40	65.8	−25.8	665.64	10.1
B	89	63.2	25.8	665.64	10.5
C	91	65.2	25.8	665.64	10.2
D	37	62.8	−25.8	665.64	10.5

5. The next step is to work out the degrees of freedom (*df*) using the following formula:

   $df = (R - 1)(C - 1)$. Remember that R stands for rows and C stands for columns. In this case $df = 1 \times 1 = 1$.

6. The next step is to check for the significance of our χ^2 value by looking this up in Table A6 in Appendix A.

7. As can be seen from our results, we have a significant χ^2 value ($p < 0.02$). How do we interpret this? If you go back to the original data table you can see that 70% of males had a conversation on their mobile phone when it rang, whereas only about 30% of females observed had a mobile phone conversation. This accounts for the significant result that was observed from this particular set of data. What you may conclude from this data is that women are more polite about using their mobile phone when they are in the company of other people.

Content analysis

The aim of content analysis is to analyse textual data and attempt to establish a set of themes or categories by 'reducing' the text into these categories and frequencies of occurrence. Therefore, content analysis reduces qualitative data into a quantified form. In order for this approach to be successful you have to ensure that you have enough material to be analysed. To help explain this more clearly, let's consider the following example in Technical Tip 8.

Technical Tip 8

Conducting a content analysis

You have just conducted a study comparing 10 people's performances when using an internet enabled PDA device. To interact with the application, participants used a stylus. After participants used the service, you asked them the following two questions:

1. *what did you like about the service?*
2. *what did you dislike about the service?*

Not all of the participants had anything to say in response to these questions (as is sometimes the case). Therefore, the responses you received to these two questions are shown in Table 8.17.

Table 8.17   Participant Interview Responses

Participant	What did you Dislike?	What did you Like?
1	I found the application, the stylus actually, really hard to use	Once, you got the hang of it, it would be good to use in crowded places
2	Even after the third task, I still didn't think the stylus was easy to use	It would be good to switch between the stylus and using the keypad, depending where you were
3	The help option isn't easy to find, so you don't know it's there and start to panic	It would be easy to use this in a crowded location
4	If you make a mistake, it's not easy to rectify it	I liked the different services that you could access using this application
5	I found it really slow	It would be good to use in places where you shouldn't really use it, like lectures. It's more discrete than using your mobile
6	If you chose an option, it took you ages to get back to where you wanted to go	I would have liked to be able to have a writing facility included in this type of application
7	I've never used anything like this before and it showed	I thought it was quite a quick service to use
8	I've never tried to use a stylus in interact with a computer screen before. That affected my performance I'm sure	I'm sure it would be easier to use once you practiced using it a bit more

1. Having gathered this data, the next step would be to examine individual responses to see if there are any patterns or themes emerging from it, by looking at all the statements carefully. What you are looking for will be related to the aims of your study. For example, are there any usability issues relating to how easy it is to use the application? Alternatively, you could look back to Chapter 4 and take Molich and Nielson's (1990) list of heuristics to help you categorise the raw data into themes.
2. After looking over the data a number of times (remember that this is a subjective process) you may begin to notice a few themes emerging.

For example, in relation to the data provided in the above example, you may notice the following themes:

- participants seemed to find it difficult to use the stylus
- if a participant made an error when interacting with the application, they found it difficult to recover from it
- participants thought the application would be really useful in certain locations
- speed of interaction was an issue for participants, they seemed to think it was too slow
- previous experience of using this type of application would help improve people's ability to use the application

3. Now that you believe that you have identified key aspects related to people's perception of the service, you should try and label these themes:

   – *Ease of use*
   – *Error recovery*
   – *Context of use*
   – *Speed of application*
   – *Previous experience*

4. In order to assess the reliability and validity of your findings you can ask another researcher to look at the raw data too and identify what they think are the themes emerging from your data. According to Miles and Huberman (1994) you can calculate the reliability of the themes identified through this process by calculating the number of times that the two researchers (or more if you've got a few willing friends) agree on themes as an overall percentage of all the possible themes that have been proposed. Miles and Huberman (1994) state that you should be chapter has been to provide you with an overview of how you might analyse the data that you have collected as part of your study aiming for an overall agreement rate of about 70%.

SUMMARY

The aim of this chapter was to give you an introduction to some of the statistical techniques that you can use when trying to interpret the data you have collected as part of your mobile HCI study. These forms of data analysis were based on data collection approaches that are discussed in Chapter 3. As stated at the start of the chapter, it is important that you choose appropriate forms of data collection before you start your study. If you don't do this, you will find it very difficult to carry out any worthwhile statistical analysis of your data; garbage in, garbage out, as the old maxim goes.

The chapter started off with a discussion on how to describe your data both numerically and in tables and diagrams. By presenting your findings in a clear and unambiguous way, interested individuals will be able to understand the results of the statistical analyses you have presented and also, hopefully, understand why you have chosen to interpret your results in a particular way.

The actual tests themselves covered aspects of parametric and non-parametric analysis ranging from testing for differences (e.g. *t*-tests, Mann-Whitney U and Wilcoxon), looking for relationships between scores (e.g. correlation analysis) and also how to analyse and interpret categorical data (e.g. content analysis, CHI-square). Although you were asked to go through and calculate the test statistics by hand, I am aware that some of you may be familiar with commercially available statistical software packages and use these to help you undertake your data analysis. However, I think it is important that you have a clear idea of why you should use a particular statistical test before you start entering your raw data into a stats package and pressing buttons. If you don't, you can end up with using the wrong tests and presenting results that do not reflect what the results are actually telling you.

Therefore, before you undertake any form of mobile HCI study you need to clearly think about the research method you will use and what form of statistical analysis you can perform on the data. To help you along the way, I've included a decision chart in Appendix C based on the statistical tests covered in this chapter.

Self test

- Related *t*-test
- Unrelated *t*-test
- Wilcoxon test
- Mann-Whitney U
- Spearman's Rho
- Pearson's Correlation Coefficient
- CHI-square
- Content Analysis

Exercises

1. You have started work as a user experience analyst for a mobile telecommunications company. For your first project you are working on a new multimedia messaging service. The project manager wants you to provide the rest of the design team with a short report detailing a method for assessing people's attitude towards the new service and also a technique for statistically analysing and interpreting the data you get back from the participants in your user experience study. The report should include a justification for the proposed research approach as well as the statistical tests chosen to analyse the data.

2. You are about to undertake an observational study investigating people's use of camera phones in public places. You have to develop a coded observation form for this study. After carrying your study, analyse the data using a CHI-square analysis.

REFERENCES

Miles, M.B. and Huberman, A.M. (1994) *Qualitative Data Analysis: an expanded sourcebook, 2nd edition.* Sage Publications, Thousand Oaks, CA

SUGGESTED FURTHER READING

Burns, R.B. (2000) *Introduction to Research Methods.* Sage Publications

Coolican, H. (2000) *Research Methods and Statistics in Psychology.* Hodder and Stoughton

Filed, A. (2000) *Discovering Statistics Using SPSS for Windows.* Sage Publications

Rowntree, D. (2003) *Statistics Without Tears: a primer for non-mathematicians.* Allyn and Bacon

Silverman, D. (2001) *Interpreting Qualitative Data: methods for analysing talk, text and interaction, 2nd edition.* Sage Publications, London

9

Conclusions

INTRODUCTION

This chapter focuses on areas for further development and research within the area of mobile HCI. The chapter will explore the impact of 3G technology and its potential effects on the development of new application domains, such as location-based services, entertainment services, healthcare, personalisation and mobile learning. In addition, this chapter will consider what kinds of research methods will need to be employed to effectively investigate not only the functional aspects of these new mobile devices services and applications but also the continuing social impact of these developing mobile technologies. This social impact, after all, is one of the major driving forces as to why people choose to use technology, and how they adapt it to their needs.

3G TECHNOLOGY

What is 3G? Essentially, 3G stands for the third generation of mobile telecommunications technology which offers an increased bandwidth to allow mobile phone operators to provide a wider and better range of services. This bandwidth should increase data transfer rates to about 2 megabits per second (with the promise of 100 megabits per second for 4G phones and the ability to move around in 3D virtual communities). For example, due to the increased bandwidth available, users will, in theory, be able to watch sporting events such as highlights from soccer matches on their phone while sitting on the train on the way home. In addition, 3G services offer the opportunity to surf the internet (with the added bonus of having an 'always on' internet connection) and have access to services such as downloadable video clips, and music as opposed to the limited services you are able to access via WAP devices. In general, WAP services are mainly text-based information services for such things as the weather, news headlines and sports results. However, with technological advances such as GPRS which is classed as an 'always-on' internet service with higher bandwidth (which we've already mentioned) users should have more reliable access to the internet and a 'media rich' environment, such as graphics, video streaming and the like (this claim, however, is currently a subject of debate amongst commentators in the general public at present in the UK, as some experts believe that you will only be able to access the internet via the portal provided by your mobile phone operator. You will not in effect have free access to roam as with the world wide web (WWW). Another feature of the 3G mobile devices will be the ability to hold videoconferences on your mobile phone (provided, of course, that the parties involved all have 3G camera phones). There is also the ability to play online games. For example, you will be able to access real-time multiplayer games, with a promise from the service providers being that these will be more realistic, due to high bandwidth and the ability to produce high resolution 3D pictures. Oh, and before I forget, you will be able to make phone calls as well. These, of course, will all be subject to the network connection coverage you have on your mobile phone or mobile device as you go from one location to another. In addition to the services provided by 3G technology, there is also the mobile device to think about too. This is an interesting consideration to make as some users often cannot easily distinguish between the phone and the network. This leads on to the question of what exactly is the user interface?

What do users want or expect in relation to the development of mobile devices and services? According to a survey recently carried out by the AvantGo Mobile Lifestyles Survey (2004), people want a device that would have the standard PDA features as well as the ability to store and play music like Apple's iPod; have a larger screen than standard mobile phones; be compact in size; and have global positioning service capability. The top 12 features of the all-in 'dream device' according to the AvantGo survey were as follows:

1. Calendar/contact list
2. Easy to synchronise with a PC

3. Great battery life
4. Email/messaging
5. Wi-Fi/Bluetooth
6. Compact size
7. MP3 player
8. Phone
9. Large screen
10. GPS locator
11. 20+ gigabyte memory
12. Camera.

It has to be said that this survey was based on a sample of people who are known in marketing terminology as 'early technology adapters'. However, history has shown that what users ask for is not what they will really use. For example, look at the actual take-up of WAP compared to its demand.

Having considered these aspects, what are the academic research areas of interest that will become hot topics for research? One of the most important areas for development will be in the area of *location-based services*.

Location-based services

What is a location-based service? Duri *et al.* (2001) define location-based services as services where the location of a person will shape or focus the application or service that the user accesses. This emphasises that in a dynamic mobile environment, the mobile device user will have changing needs and requirements. According to some reports in the press, location-based services will account for over 40% of mobile phone operators' data services revenue by 2007. Given the size of this figure, it is crucial that the product developers get their designs correct. The idea behind this is for services to be provided to the user in a mobile context in relation to what specific location you find yourself in, e.g. you may have arrived in town and want to find out where the nice restaurants, pubs and museums are. Factors that will have to be taken into consideration in relation to the development of these services include:

- Limited input styles
- Screen size
- Wireless connections (e.g. Wifi, WLAN, UMTS, GPRS and GSM)
- Reduced information complexity.

A crucial aspect for the development of mobile services and applications is their context of use. Preece *et al.* (p. 207, 2002) define context of use as 'the circumstances in which the interactive product is expected to operate', and include the social, technological, organisational and physical environment. These are the key elements that one should be aware of when undertaking *any* form of mobile HCI research. What does this mean for location-based services?

Let's start with the social dimension to context of use. We have already seen in chapter 6 that people have expectations about the use of technology in public places, and as 3G service develops and is rolled out by the service providers, there will need to be further research work undertaken to assess the social impact of this new form of technology. For example, will people want to use a location-based service about booking a table in a restaurant whilst sitting in a busy, noisy bus using speech as opposed to keypad entry? In addition, how reliable are wireless connections that allow people to connect to various services whilst they are on the go? For example, I've tried to use my laptop wireless connection on the train and it is often difficult to get a constant connection. This is also not an uncommon problem if you use your mobile phone to make a call on the train (the organisational aspect is something that we also discussed in Chapter 6). Therefore, how will mobile devices change the dynamics of work for the mobile worker, how can they be made to feel part of an organisation, or part of a team and not feel isolated? In addition, they will need access to various kinds of information whilst they are mobile in order to carry out their job. It is crucial therefore that the information is presented to the mobile worker that reflects the dynamic environment that they work in. For example, it may not always be possible to use speech input and so the service should allow the mobile worker to switch to keypad entry.

Research methods

Kjeldskov and Graham (2003) highlighted the fact that the majority of research conducted in relation to mobile HCI is still carried out in a laboratory setting. There are benefits for conducting mobile HCI research in the lab, as we saw in Chapter 4 (e.g. carrying out preliminary research on a prototypical interface), but more research has to be conducted in the dynamic context of the real world where these applications and devices will actually be used. This will require researchers and designers to think about using some of the techniques that we discussed in Chapter 4, such as observational studies and field work. This is necessary in order to increase the ecological validity (remember that phrase?) of any research findings that are produced.

Education

Mobile learning is a term that you may hear a lot more of in the coming years. What does it mean? It means using devices such as PDAs, laptops, tablet PCs and even mobile phones in teaching and learning environments.

Why should mobile learning become an area of interest? The use of mobile devices such as PDAs or tablet PCs offer an opportunity to enhance the learning environment for students. In addition to this, there are also logistical and cost benefits. For example, due to their size, mobile devices can be used in a normal-sized classroom without the need to go and book a dedicated computer or ICT suite. It also means that students are not hidden behind their PC monitor, and can easily interact with the teacher and other pupils in the class. In terms of cost, mobile devices – like mobile phones and PDAs – are more reasonably priced than desktops and can offer most of the functionality that a desktop PC can offer in terms of the needs of these applications and services.

So what are the learning benefits that we should be considering? A psychologist called Vygotsky (1978) stated that social facilitation is a crucial element in learning, and promoted the idea of collaborative learning in the classroom. According to Cohen (1994), effective collaborative learning activities include individual and group achievement, cooperation and interaction to achieve shared goals, designated roles and rules. So learning is not just something that students can do on their own. Research has shown (e.g. Lou *et al.*, 2001) that computer-supported collaborative learning (CSCL) tools, whereby information communication technologies are used in a classroom/teaching environment, has provided new opportunities for achieving these collaborative learning conditions. However, as Inkpen *et al.* (1999) pointed out, due to the traditionally desk-bound nature of these interactions, that collaborative learning opportunities have been limited. Some research (e.g. Mandryk *et al.*, 2001) seems to suggest that mobile devices such as PDAs and technological advances in relation to WLANS, can provide the opportunity for effective face-to-face interaction between both teacher–pupil and pupil–pupil relationships. For example, Zurita *et al.* (2003) report on a controlled experimental study that they conducted looking at two groups of school pupils who were given a collaborative learning maths-based exercise. One group of pupils used wireless handheld devices. The other group of students did not use any form of ICT support. The results of this study found that the students who carried out the exercise using the handheld devices learned more than the other group of students. The reasons for this were put down to aspects such as improving social interaction between the pupils, and more smoothly coordinating the synchronisation of activities between pupils.

Even at university level, we can find examples of mobile devices enhancing the learning environment. For example, in the USA, medical schools are leading the way in using handheld devices and wireless technology to their benefit. The advantages are seen as being an improvement in student–teacher communication, and the fact that students can have access to the latest up to date information as they move between classrooms or hospital wards as part of their training. According to Fallon (2002) about 20 per cent of the country's medical schools in the US require their third- and fourth-year medical students to carry handheld computers.

For any pedagogical success (i.e. effective learning) to take place, it is also crucial that both teachers and pupils are given enough time to familiarise themselves with the devices they will be using in the learning environment before any formal teaching takes place. On the teachers' side, this includes not only being familiar with the technological capabilities of the devices themselves, but also how the devices will support the specific learning goals that they have in mind. This implies that teachers themselves have to develop learning outcomes with the mobile devices in mind right from the start, rather than trying to fit their application into their normal, non-mobile learning goals and teaching techniques.

Apart from the pedagogical benefits, mobile technology offers other benefits to mobile learning. For example, as the majority of students now own mobile phones (at least in the affluent developed countries), the university can harness this information by sending students information regarding timetables (or sudden timetable changes), exam dates (or reminders of exam dates!) and deadline reminders for coursework. It could also be used as a form of getting urgent information to students (e.g. contact home due to a sudden illness of a loved one). In addition, whilst on campus, students could use the WLAN to get information on the library opening hours, renew books from the library, request books, and even browse the library catalogue from the comfort of a student café.

Healthcare

The area of healthcare is another domain where great advances are beginning to be made in relation to mobile ICT use, as can be seen from the example above in relation to medical training in hospitals. However, mobile devices and wireless technology offer other opportunities to healthcare professionals. Consider again the mobile health worker (e.g. a district nurse) who is making a home visit. They will need to get up-to-date access to the records of the patient they are visiting, and they will have to make sure that they can have the wireless connectivity that they need to update records and search for information needed in relation to the patient's condition. Beyond this, they may have to try to arrange a case conference with other medical healthcare workers involved (e.g. general practitioner, social worker) with a particular patient whilst they are on the move. In addition, they may want to have the facility to email the pharmacist a new prescription that the patient can pick up. Therefore, it is important for designers to have a clear understanding of the changing needs of the mobile health worker due to the dynamic environment they operate in and accommodate these in the system design.

Personalisation

Personalisation of mobile devices and applications will continue to develop. For example, we have all been amused when the person sitting next to us on the train suddenly reaches into their pocket to retrieve a mobile phone that is playing a particular cheesy tune (in our opinion of course). The business of personalised ring tones is a very lucrative market for mobile phone companies and other providers of this service. In addition, it is not uncommon to see people changing the cover of their mobile phone to match the outfit they are wearing or perhaps reflecting their current mood. Perhaps we could also see the same with changes to the interface, as well as to the look of the device itself. This offers an interesting challenge to user interface designers.

Personalisation, in relation to the types of services that people want to have access to via their mobile phones and mobile devices, is now possible. For example, people can register to have alerts sent to them via their mobile phone informing them of their team's latest score in a soccer match (although if you are a Scotland fan, speaking from personal experience, this can have a negative impact on your mood and those sitting with you).

Personalisation should also encompass the ability of individuals to interact with mobile devices in ways that accommodate their particular needs. For example (as we saw in the chapter on individual differences – Chapter 2), it is important that specific groups who are often ignored in the design process, such as older users and people who have poor eyesight or hearing difficulty, can personalise their mobile device to allow them to have an effective, efficient and satisfying experience. This may include the ability to have larger font sizes set up as the default for their mobile phone or PDA, or the ability to switch easily between speech and touch-tone input.

SUMMARY

The aim of this chapter was to provide you with some ideas about where the developments in mobile services and research areas may be heading. These included entertainment services such as multi-player gaming and watching highlights of soccer matches on your mobile phone whilst you are on the train on the way home, and developments in the educational setting with mobile devices being used to help improve collaborative learning. In addition, we also looked at location-based services such as tourist information guides and other services that meet the needs of users in the current context of where they are located (e.g. local bus and train timetable information). Personalisation is another area that will continue to develop as service providers study our patterns of use for our mobile devices – you may find that you end up getting more commercial 'spam' sent to your mobile device than your desktop as service providers try to chase the lucrative mobile user market. A more positive aspect of personalisation will be the opportunity for groups of users (e.g. older users and people with hearing and visual difficulties) being able to adapt their mobile device interfaces to meet their needs. In addition, it is to be hoped that service providers also tailor the presentation of their service content to reflect the needs of these groups of users.

Overall, this book has been designed to give you an introduction and overview of the various factors that contribute to the area of mobile HCI. I hope you have found it reasonably informative. The next step is for you to go out and watch people using mobile technology and get ideas about projects that you can undertake to help contribute to our knowledge of this fascinating area of research. Good luck.

Self test

- Location-based services
- Computer supported collaborative learning
- Personalisation
- Context of use

Exercises

1. What context of use factors should you take into consideration when designing a tourist information guide for mobile devices such as a mobile phone?

2. Develop a computer supported collaborative learning exercise that teaches people how to create a prototype for a context-aware tourist information guide for a PDA.

REFERENCES

AvantGo Mobile Lifestyles Survey (2004) http://www.ianywhere.com/press_releases/avantgo_dreams_survey.html. Accessed 11.01.05

Cohen, E.G. (1994) Restructuring the Classroom: conditions for productive small groups. *Review of Educational Research*, **64**(1), 1–35

Duri, S., Cole, A., Munson, J. and Chritsensen, J. (2001) An approach to providing a seamless end-user experience for location-aware applications. *Proceedings of 1st International Workshop on Mobile Commerce*, Rome, Italy, pp. 20–25

Fallon, M. (2002) Handheld Devices: towards a more mobile campus. http://www.campus-technology.com/print.asp?ID=6896. Accessed 04.01.05

Inkpen, K.M., Ho-Ching, W., Kuederle, O., Scott, S.D. and Shoemaker, G. (1999) This is fun! We're all best friends and we're all playing: supporting children's synchronous collaboration. *Proceedings of Computer Supported Collaborative Learning (CSCL) '99*, Stanford, CA

Kjeldskov, J. and Graham, C. (2003) A review of mobile HCI research methods. In *Proceedings of 5th International Symposium, Mobile HCI*, L. Chittaro (Ed.), pp. 317–335. Springer

Lou, Y., Abrami, P.C. and d'Apollonia, S. (2001) Small group and individual learning with technology: a meta-analysis. *Review of Educational Research*, **71**(3), 449–521

Mandryk, R.L., Inkpen, K.M., Bilezikjian, M., Kleemer, S.R. and Landay, J.A. (2001) Supporting children's collaboration across handheld computers. In *Extended Abstracts of CHI, Conference of Human Factors in Computing Systems*. Seattle, USA, 2001

Preece, J., Rogers, Y.R. and Sharp, H. (2002) *Interaction Design: beyond human–computer interaction*. John Wiley and Sons

Vygotsky, L. (1978) *Mind in Society: the development of higher psychological processes*. Cambridge: Harvard University Press

Zurita, G., Nussbaum, M. and Shaples, M. (2003) Encouraging face-to-face collaboration learning through the use of handheld computers in the classroom. In *Proceedings of 5th International Symposium, Mobile HCI*, L. Chittaro (Ed.), pp. 193–208. Springer

SUGGESTED FURTHER READING

Harper, R. (2003) People versus information: the evolution of mobile technology. In *Proceedings of 5th International Symposium, Mobile HCI*, L. Chittaro (Ed.), pp. 1–14. Springer

Rheingold, H. (2002) *Smart Mobs: the next social revolution*. Perseus Publishing

References

Ager, J. (2003) *In Constant Touch: a global history of the mobile telephone*. Icon books, UK

Andre, T.S. (2001) The user action framework: a reliable foundation for usability engineering support tools. *International Journal of Human-Computer Studies*, **54**, pp. 107–136. London: Academic Press

Argyle, M., Furnham, A. and Graham, J.A. (1981) *Social Situations*. Cambridge University Press

Atkinson, R.L., Atkinson, R.C. and Hilgard, E.R. (1983) *Introduction to Psychology*, Harcourt Brace Janovich

AvantGo Mobile Lifestyles Survey (2004). http://www.ianywhere.com/press_releases/avantgo_dreams_survey.html. Accessed 11-01-05

Baddeley, A.D. and Hitch, G. (1974) Working memory. In *Recent Advances in Learning and Motivation*. Bower, G.A. (Ed.). Academic Press: New York

Bailey, R.W. (2001) Heuristic evaluation versus user testing. UI design update newsletter – January 2001. http://www.humanfactors.com/library/jan001.htm

Barber, C. (2001) An interactive heuristic evaluation toolkit. Master's Project, University of Sussex, UK. http://www.id-book.com/catherb/index.htm

Barnard, E., Halberstadt, A., Kotelly, C. and Phillips, M. (1999) A consistent approach to designing spoken-dialogue systems. In *Proceedings of the Automatic Speech Recognition and Understanding Workshop*. Keystone, CO: USA

Baum, F. (1900) *The Wizard of Oz*. Collins, London

Blattner, M.M., Sumikawa, D.A. and Greenberg, R.M. (1989) Earcons and icons: their structure and common design principles. *Human-Computer Interaction*, **4**(1), 11–44

Brewster, S.A. (1997) Navigating telephone-based interfaces with earcons. In *Proceedings of BCS HCI* 1997, Bristol, UK, pp. 39–56

Brewster, S.A. (2002) Overcoming the lack of screen space on mobile computers. *Personal and Ubiquitous Computing*, 6, 188–205

Bristow, G. (1986) The speech recognition problem. In *Electric Speech Recognition*, Bristow, G. (Ed.), Collins

BT Cellnet (2001) Mobile Etiquette: Changing the way we use our mobiles. http://www.btcellnet.net/cgi-bin accessed 15/10/01

Burns, T. (1992) *Erving Goffman*. London: Routledge

Carroll, J.B. (1993) *Human Cognitive Abilities: a survey of factor-analytic studies.* Cambridge University Press, New York

Carver, C.S. and Scheier, M.F. (1992) *Perspectives on Personality.* Allyn and Bacon

Chen, C., Czerwinski, M. and Macredie, R. (2000) Individual differences in virtual environments – introduction and overview. *Journal of the American Society for Information Science,* **51**(6), 499–507

Cohen, E.G. (1994) Restructuring the classroom: conditions for productive small groups. *Review of Educational Research,* **64**(1), 1–35

Coolican, H. (2000) *Introduction to Research Methods and Statistics in Psychology,* 3rd edition. Hodder and Stoughton

Coolican, H. (2000) *Research Methods and Statistics in Psychology.* Hodder and Stoughton

Cooper, A. (1999) *TheIinmates are Running the Asylum.* SAMS Publishing, Indianapolis, IN

Egan, D. (1988) Individual differences in human-computer interaction. In *Handbook of Human-Computer Interaction,* Helander, M. (Ed.). Elsevier Science Publishers: North Holland, pp. 543–568

Egan, D.E. and Gomez, L.M. (1985) Assaying, isolating and accommodating individual differences in learning a complex skill. In *Individual Differences in Cognition,* Dillon, R.F. (Ed.). Academic Press: Orlando, pp. 173–217

Ericsson, K.A. and Simon, H.A. (1985) *Protocol Analysis: verbal reports as data.* Cambridge MA: MIT Press

Fallon, M. (2002) Handheld devices: towards a more mobile campus. http://www.campus-technology.com/print.asp?ID=6896. Accessed 04.01.05

Fiske, S. (1995) Social Cognition. In *Advanced Social Psychology,* Tesser, A. (Ed.). pp. 149–194. New York: McGraw-Hill

Fortunanti, L. (2001) The mobile phone: an identity on the move, *Personal and Ubiquitous and Personal Computing,* **5**(2), 85–98

Fraser, N.M. and Gilbert, G.N. (1990) Simulating speech systems. *Computer Speech and Language,* **5**(1), 81–90

Gifford, R. (1987) *Environmental Psychology: Principles and Practice.* Boston: Allyn

Goffman, E. (1959) *The Presentation of Self in Everyday Life.* New York: Doubleday

Goldberg, L.R. (1981) Language and individual differences: the search for universals in personality lexicons. In *Perspectives in Personality,* Carver, C.S. and Scheier, M.F. (Eds.), Allyn and Bacon

Goodman, J., Brewster, S. and Gray, P. (2004) Older people, mobile devices and navigation. *Proceedings of the workshop on HCI and the Older Population,* Goodman, J. and Brewster, S. (Eds.), 7th September 2004 BCS HCI 2004, Leeds, UK

Goodman, J., Syme, A. and Eisma, R. (2003) Age-old question(naire)s. *Proceedings of Include 2003,* UK

Gregor, P., Newell, A. and Zajicek, M. (2002) Designing for dynamic diversity-interfaces for older people. In: *Proceedings of the Fifth International ACM conference on Assistive Technologies (ASSETS 2002)*, Edinburgh, UK, 8–10 July 2002

Hall, E.T. (1966) *The Hidden Dimension: Man's Use of Space in Public and Private*. Bodley Head: London

Harper, R. (2003) People versus information: the evolution of mobile technology. In *Proceedings of 5th International Symposium, Mobile HCI*, L Chittaro (Ed.), pp. 1–14. Springer

Harper, R., Randall, D. and Rouncefield, M. (2000) *Organisational Change and Retail Finance: An Ethnographic Perspective*. London: Routeledge

Hauptmann, A.G. (1989) Speech and gestures for graphic image manipulation. I, *Proceedings of CHI 1989*, Austin, Texas, USA, pp. 241–245

Heim, A.W. (1970) *AH4 Group Test of General Intelligence*, NFER, UK

Hitch, G. and Baddeley, A.D. (1976) Verbal reasoning and working memory, *Quarterly Journal of Experimental Psychology*, **28**, 603–621

Inkpen, K.M., Ho-Ching, W., Kuederle, O., Scott, S.D. and Shoemaker, G. (1999) This is fun! We're all best friends and we're all playing: supporting children's synchronous collaboration. *Proceedings of Computer Supported Collaborative Learning (CSCL) '99*, Stanford, CA

Ito, M. (2001) Mobile phones, Japanese youth, and the re-placement of social contact. In *Proceedings of Annual Meeting for the Society for the Social Studies of Science*. Cambridge, MA

ITU (2003) Mobile cellular, subscribers per 100 people. http://www.itu.int/ITUD/ict/statistics. Accessed 11.01.05

Jung, C. (1971) *Psychological Types*. Kegan Paul Harcourt Brace and Co.

Katz, J. and Aarkhus, M. (Eds.) (2002) *Perpetual contact: mobile communication, private talk, public performance*. Cambridge University Press, UK

Kaya, N. and Erkíp, F. (1999) Invasion of personal space under the condition of short-term crowding: a case study on an automatic teller machine. *Journal of Environmental Psychology*, **19**, 183–189

Keates, S. and Clarkson, P.J. (2002) Defining design inclusion. In Keates, S. *et al.* (Eds.) *Universal Access and Assistive Technology*, Springer, Berlin, Heidelberg, New York

Kjeldskov, J. and Graham, C. (2003) A review of mobile HCI research methods. In *Proceedings of 5th International Symposium, Mobile HCI*, L Chittaro (Ed.), pp. 317–335. Springer

Koubek, R.J., LeBould, W.K. and Salvendy, G. (1985) Predicting performance in computer programming courses, *Behaviour and Information Technology*, **4**(2), 12–129

Labrador, C. and Dinesh, P. (1984) Experiments in speech interaction with conversational data services. In *Proceedings of INTERACT 1984*, London, UK, pp. 104–108

Leplatre, G. and Brewter, S.A. (2000) Designing non-speech sounds to support navigation in mobile phone menus. In *Proceedings of ICAD 2000*, Atlanta, USA, pp. 190–199

Lines, L and Hone, K.S. (2004) Eliciting user requirements with older adults: lessons from the design of an interactive domestic alarm system. *Universal Access in the Information Society*, **3**(2), 141–148

Ling, R. (2002) 'The social juxtaposition of mobile telephone conversations and public spaces. In *The Social consequences of mobile telephones*, Kim, S.D. (Ed.), Chunchon, Korea

Ling, R. (2004) *The Mobile Connection: the cell phone's impact on society.* Morgan Kaufmann, San Francisco, CA

Lohman, D.F. (1989) Human intelligence: an introduction to advances in theory and research. *Review of Educational Research*, **59**(4), 333–373

Longoria, R. (Ed) (2004) *Designing Software for the Mobile Context: a practioner's guide.* Springer

Lou, Y. Abrami, P.C. and d'Apollonia, S. (2001) Small group and individual learning with technology: a meta-analysis. *Review of Educational Research*, **71**(3), 449–521

Love, S. (2001) Space Invaders: Do Mobile Phone Conversations Invade Peoples' Personal Space? *Proceedings of the18th International Human Factors in Telecommunications Symposium* in Bergen, Norway, 5–7 November 2001, pp. 125–131

Love, S., Foster, J.C. and Jack, M.A. (1997) Assaying and isolating individual difference in automated telephone services. *Proceedings of the 16th International Symposium on Human Factors in Telecommunications (HFT '97)*, pp. 323–330

Love, S., Foster, J.C. and Jack, M.A. (1997) Assaying and isolating individual differences in automated telephone services. *Proceedings of the 16th International Conference on Human Factors in Telecommunications (HFT '97)*, pp. 323–330

Love, S., Foster, J.C. and Jack, M.A. (2000) Health warning: use of speech synthesis can cause personality changes. *State of the Art in Speech Synthesis*, pp. 14/1–14/8, IEE Publications, Savoy Place, London, UK

Mandryk, R.L., Inkpen, K.M., Bilezikjian, M., Kleemer, S.R. and Landay, J.A. (2001) Supporting children's collaboration across handheld computers. In *Extended Abstracts of CHI, Conference of Human Factors in Computing Systems*. Seattle, USA, 2001

Marcus, A. (2002) Metaphors and user interfaces in the 21st century. *Interactions*, **9**(2), 7–10

McCrae, R.R. and Costa, P.T. (1987) Validation of the five-factor model of personality across instruments and observers. *Journal of Personality and Social Psychology*, **52**, 81–90

Molich, R. and Nielson, J. (1990) Improving a human-computer dialogue. *Communications of the ACM,* **33**(3), 338–348

Monk, A., Wright, P., Haber, J. and Davenport, L. (1993a) *Improving your Human-Computer Interface: a practical technique.* New York: Prentice Hall

Morgan, K. and Macleod, H. (1990) The possible role of personality factors in computer interface preference. In *Second Interdisciplinary Workshop on Mental Models,* Robinson College, Cambridge

Murtagh, G. (2000) Seeing the 'Rules': Preliminary Observations of action, Interaction and Mobile Phone Use. In *Wireless World: Social and Interactional Aspects of the Mobile Age,* Brown, B., Green, N. and Harper, R. (Eds.). London: Springer

Neilson, J. (1993) *Usability Engineering.* Cambridge, MA: Academic Press

Nielson, J. (1994) Heuristic Evaluation. In *Usability Inspection Methods.* John Wiley, New York

Nielson, J. and Landauer, T.K. (1993) A mathematical model of finding of usability problems. *Proceedings of INTERACT 1993,* pp. 206–213. New York: Academic Press

Norman, D.A. (1999) *The Design of Everyday Things,* MIT Press

Noyes, J. (2001) Talking and writing – how natural in human-machine interaction? *International Journal of Human-Computer Studies,* **55**(4), 503–519

Openwave phone simlulator software, http://developer.openwave.com/dvl. Accessed 13.01.05

Palen, L., Salzman, M. and Youngs, E. (2000) Going Wireless: behaviour and Practice of New Mobile Phone Users. In *Proceeding of the ACM 2000 Conference on Computer Supported Cooperative Work,* Philadelphia, PA, pp. 201–210. New York: ACM Press

Pitt, I. and Edwards, A. (2003) *Design of Speech-based Devices.* Springer

Poulsen, P.G., Lewis, C., Rieman, J. and Wharton, C. (1992) Cognitive walk-throughs: a method for theory-based evaluation of users interfaces. *International Journal of Man-Machine Studies,* **36**, 741–773

Preece, J., Rogers, Y., Benyon, D., Holland, S. and Carey, T. (1994) *Human-Computer Interaction.* Addison-Wesley, Chapter 2, pp. 29–52

Preece, J., Rogers, Y.R. and Sharp, H. (2002) *Interaction Design: beyond human-computer interaction.* John Wiley and Sons

Reeves, B. and Nash, C. (1999) *The Media Equation: how people treat computers, television, and new media like real people and places.* Cambridge University Press, New York

Rheingold, H. (2002) *Smart Mobs: the next social revolution.* Perseus Publishing, Cambridge, MA

Schmandt, C. (1987) Conversational telecommunications environments. In *Cognitive Engineering in the Design of Human-Computer Interaction and Expert Systems,* Salvendy, G. (Ed.). Elsevier Science

Sears, O.D., Peplau, A. and Freedman, J. (1988), *Social Psychology*. New York: Prentice Hall

Sharp, J., Peters, J. and Howard K. (2002) *The Management of a Student Research Project*, 3rd edition. Gower

Silverman, D. (2001) *Interpreting Qualitative Data: methods for analysing, talk, text and interaction*. Sage Publications, London

Smith, D.C., Irby, C., Kimball, R., Verplank, B. and Harslem, E. (1982) Designing the Star User Interface. *Byte*, **7**(4), 242–282

Souvignier, V., Kellner, A., Rueber, B., Schramm, H. and Seide, F. (2000) The thoughtful elephant: strategies for spoken dialogue systems. *IEEE Transactions of Speech and Audio Process*, **8**(1), 51–62

Stanney, K. and Salvendy, G. (1995) Information visualisation: assisting low spatial individuals with information access tasks through the use of visual mediators. *Ergonomics*, **38**(6), 1184–1198

Taylor, A. and Harper, R. (2002) Age-old practices in the 'new world': a study of gift-giving between teenage mobile phone users. In *Proceedings of CHI 2002*, pp. 135–446. NY: ACM Press

Tun, P.A. and Wingfield, A. (1997) Language and communication: fundamentals of speech communication and language processing in old age. In *Handbook of human factors and the older adult*, Fisk, A.D. and Rogers, W.A. (Eds.), Academic Press, San Diego

Turkle, S. (1984) *The Second Self: computers and the human spirit*. Granada Publishing

Vaananen-Vainio-Mattila, K. and Ruska, S. (2000). Designing mobile phones and communicators for consumers' needs at Nokia. In Eric Bergman (Ed.) *Information Appliances and Beyond, Interaction Design for Consumer Products*. San Francisco, USA: Mogan Kaufmann

Veitch, R. and Arkkelin, D. (1995) *Environmental Psychology: An Interdisciplinary Perspective*, New York: Prentice Hall

Vicente, K. and Williges, R. (1988) Accommodating individual differences in searching a hierarchical file system. *International Journal of Man-Machine Studies*, **29**, 647–668

Vicente, K.J., Hayes, B.C. and Williges, R.C. (1988) Assaying and isolating individual differences in searching a hierarchical file system. *Human Factors*, **29**, 349–359

Vygotsky, L. (1978) *Mind in Society: the development of higher psychological processes*. Cambridge. Harvard University Press

Watson, O.M. and Graves, T.D. (1966) Quantitative research in proxemic behaviour. *American Anthropology*, **68**, pp. 971–985. Cited in Eysenck, M.W. (2000), *Psychology: A Student's Handbook*, The Psychology Press Ltd

Wei, R. and Leung, L. (1999) Blurring public and private behaviours in public space: policy challenges in the use and improper use of the cell phone. *Telematics and Informatics*, **16**, 11–26

Weiss, S. (2002) *Handheld Usability*. John Wiley and Sons

Wollman, N., Kelly, B.M. and Bordens, K.S. (1994) Environmental and intrapersonalpredictors of reactions to potential territorial intrusions in the workplace. *Environment and Behaviour*, **26**, 179–194

Zajicek, M. and Brewster, S. (2004) A new research agenda for older adults. *Special Issue of Universal Access in the Information Society*. Volume 3, 2 June 2004

Zajicek, M. and Hall, S. (2000) *Solutions for Visually Impaired People using the Internet*. BCS HCI Sunderland 2000, pp. 299–307

Zajicek, M. and Morrisey, W. (2001) Spoken message length for older adults. *Proceedings of INTERACT 2001*, pp. 789–790

Zurita, G., Nussbaum, M. and Shaples, M. (2003) Encouraging face-to-face collaboration learning through the use of handheld computers in the classroom. In *Proceedings of 5th International Symposium, Mobile HCI*, L Chittaro (Ed.), pp. 193–208. Springer

ADDITIONAL REFERENCES

Burns, R.B. (2000) *Introduction to research methods*. Sage Publications.

Field, A. (2000) *Discovering statistics using SPSS for Windows*. Sage Publications.

Howell, M.D., Love, S. and Turner, M. (2005) Spatial metaphors for a speech-based mobile city guide service. *Journal of Personal and Ubiquitous Computing*, **9**, 32–45

Maguire, M.C. (2001a) Methods to support human-centred design. *International Journal of Human-Computer Studies*, **55**(4), 587–634

Maguire, M.C. (2001b) Context of use within usability activities. *International Journal of Human-Computer Studies*, **55**, 453–483.

McDonald, J.E. and Schv aneveldt, R.W. (1988) The application of user knowledge to interface design. In *Cognitive science and its applications for human-computer interaction*. Guindon, R. (Ed.). Hillsadale: Lawrence Erlbaum, pp. 289–338.

Osborn, A.F. (1963) *Applied imagination*. New York: Schribeners and sons

Rosenfeld, L. and Morville, P. (1998) *Information architecture for the world wide web*. Cambridge: O'Reilly

Rowntree, D. (2003) *Statistics without tears: a primer for non-mathematicians*. Allyn and Bacon.

Appendix A:
Critical value tables

Table A1   Critical Values of *t*

Degrees of freedom N =	Level of significance for a one-tailed test		
	0.05	0.025	0.005
	Level of significance for a two-tailed test		
	0.10	0.05	0.01
1	6.314	12.706	63.657
2	2.920	4.303	9.925
3	2.353	3.182	5.841
4	2.132	2.776	4.604
5	2.015	2.571	4.032
6	1.943	2.447	3.707
7	1.895	2.365	3.499
8	1.860	2.306	3.355
9	1.833	2.262	3.250
10	1.812	2.228	3.169
11	1.796	2.201	3.106
12	1.782	2.179	3.055
13	1.771	2.160	3.012
14	1.761	2.145	2.977
15	1.753	2.131	2.947
16	1.746	2.120	2.921
17	1.740	2.110	2.898
18	1.734	2.101	2.878

Remember: calculated *t* must be equal to 2 or exceed the critical value for the result to be significant at the level shown.

Table A2   Critical value of W

Degrees of freedom N =	Level of significance for a one-tailed test		
	0.05	0.025	0.01
	Level of significance for a two-tailed test		
	0.10	0.05	0.002
1	–	–	–
2	–	–	–
3	–	–	–
4	–	–	–
5	–	–	–
6	2	0	–
7	3	2	–
8	5	3	–
9	8	5	–
10	11	8	0

Remember: calculated W must be equal to or less than the critical value for the result to be significant at the level shown.

Table A3   Critical values for U

n^2	n^1									
	1	2	3	4	5	6	7	8	9	10
1	–	–	–	–	–	–	–	–	–	–
2	–	–	–	–	–	–	–	0	0	0
3	–	–	–	–	0	1	1	2	2	3
4	–	–	–	0	1	2	3	4	4	5
5	–	–	0	1	2	3	5	6	7	8
6	–	–	1	2	3	5	6	8	10	11
7	–	–	1	3	5	6	8	10	12	14
8	–	0	2	4	6	8	10	13	15	17
9	–	0	2	4	7	10	12	15	17	20
10	–	0	3	5	8	11	14	17	20	23

NB: This table represents the critical values for U for a one tailed-test at 0.025 and a two-tailed test at 0.05.
Remember: calculated U must be equal to or less than the critical value for the result to be significant at the level shown.

Table A4 Critical values for Pearson's r

Degrees of freedom = $N-2$	Level of significance for a one-tailed test		
	0.05	0.025	0.005
	Level of significance for a two-tailed test		
	0.10	0.05	0.01
2	0.9000	0.9500	0.9900
3	0.805	0.878	0.9587
4	0.729	0.811	0.9172
5	0.669	0.754	0.875
6	0.621	0.707	0.834
7	0.582	0.666	0.798
8	0.549	0.632	0.765
9	0.521	0.602	0.735
10	0.497	0.576	0.708

Remember: calculated r must be equal to or exceed the critical value for the result to be significant at the level shown.

Table A5   Critical values for Spearman's *r*

Degrees of freedom N =	Level of significance for a one-tailed test		
	0.05	0.025	0.01
	Level of significance for a two-tailed test		
	0.10	0.05	0.02
2	–	–	–
3	–	–	–
4	–	–	–
5	0.900	1.000	1.000
6	0.829	0.886	0.943
7	0.714	0.786	0.893
8	0.643	0.738	0.833
9	0.600	0.700	0.783
10	0.564	0.648	0.745

Remember: calculated *r* must be equal to or exceed the critical value for the result to be significant at the level shown.

Table A6   Critical values of χ^2

Degrees of freedom $N =$	Level of significance for a one-tailed test		
	0.05	0.025	0.01
	Level of significance for a two-tailed test		
	0.10	0.05	0.02
1	2.71	3.84	5.41
2	4.60	5.99	7.82
3	6.25	7.82	9.84
4	7.78	9.49	11.67
5	9.24	11.07	13.39
6	10.64	12.59	15.03
7	12.02	14.07	16.62
8	13.36	15.51	18.17
9	14.68	16.92	19.68
10	15.99	18.31	21.16

Remember: calculated χ^2 must be equal to or exceed the critical value for the result to be significant at the level shown.

Appendix B:
What test shall I use?

This chart will hopefully allow you to work out what test you should use based on the statistical tests that are covered in Chapter 8.

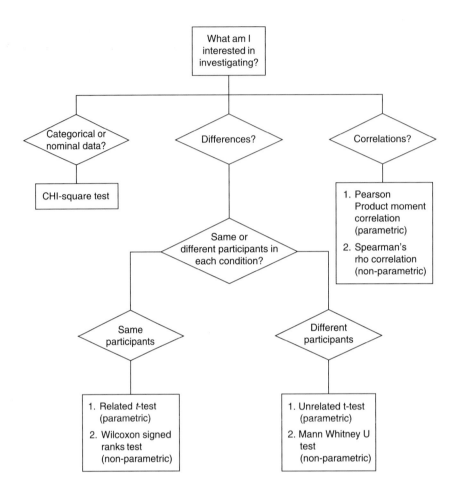

Appendix C:
Useful HCI resources

JOURNALS

Behaviour and Information Technology
Communications of the ACM
Computers in Human Behaviour
Ergonomics
Human Factors
Information Technology and People
International Journal of Human-Computer Studies
International Journal of Human-Computer Interaction
Interacting with Computers
Personal and Ubiquitous Computing
Transactions on Computer-Human Interaction
Universal Access in the Information Society

Conference Proceedings

Assistive Technologies (ASSETS)
CHI
British HCI
HCI International
Interact
Mobile HCI
NordCHI
Ubiquitous Computing (UbiComp)

INTERNET

British Computer Society HCI group: http://www.bcs-hci.org.uk/
HCI Bibliography: www.hcibib.org/
HCI Index: http://degraaff.org/hci/
Humourous look at bad UI designs: www.baddesigns.com/
Jakob Nielson's alertbox column: www.useit.com/alertbox/
Usable Web: www.usableweb.com/

Index